VENTURE CAPITAL & BUYOUTS

Brian Coyle

CIB PUBLISHING

FINANCIAL EDUCATION

CIB Publishing
c/o The Chartered Institute of Bankers
Emmanuel House
4-9 Burgate Lane
Canterbury
Kent
CT1 2XJ
United Kingdom

Telephone: 01227 762600

CIB Publishing publications are published by The Chartered Institute of Bankers, a non-profit making registered educational charity.

Typeset by The Foundry
Printed by WBC Book Manufacturers, Bridgend

ISBN 0-85297-461-2

Contents

1

Venture Capital

In broad terms, venture capital is an investment, usually in small private companies to finance their start-up, expansion, survival or change of ownership. However, venture capital is occasionally invested in large companies to support a management buyout or buy-in. The main return on venture capital investments usually is capital gain rather than dividend yield; however, the investment will be lost if the business fails. In contrast to the equity financing of large and well-established businesses, venture capital is high risk, because

- the possibility of business failure is high, and
- even if the business is successful, the investment is illiquid. Shares in a private company are not easily resold, and their value consequently will be less than the market price of shares in a comparable quoted company.

Why is Venture Capital Needed?

Venture capital is often required by a business at a critical stage in its development, for example when it is planning to expand its product range or start selling into new markets. Its existing owners or prospective purchasers might be unable to provide all the risk finance themselves and banks might be unwilling to lend as much as the business needs, because of the high credit risk.

Venture capital firms often work in conjunction with other providers of finance in putting together a total funding package for a business. Venture capital is a medium- to long-term investment, of not just money, but of time and effort. The venture capital firm's aim is to enable growth companies to develop into the major businesses of tomorrow.

Venture Capital Providers

The term venture capital usually is associated with funds provided to companies by venture capital organizations. However, venture capital could be invested directly in a business by a wealthy individual (a business angel) or by any organization. Venture capital has two main distinguishing features:

- it is provided by one or more external investors
- it is risk capital.

Venture capital is provided by an external investor, rather than by the owners or the management of the business. The external finance supplements the money invested in a business by its original owner or management team. The amount of money invested as venture capital is usually much greater than the investment of the entrepreneurs/managers; however, it is also usual for the financing package to be structured so that the entrepreneurs/managers of the business have a sizeable equity stake.

A venture capital organization often will seek to protect (and enhance) its investment by maintaining a close association with the company, often by appointing a nominee to the board of directors.

Because venture capital is risk capital, the finance provider expects to share in the profits if the company is a success, as well as to bear the loss if the company fails. Typically, a venture capital organization will provide funds as a mixture of ordinary shares, preference shares and unsecured loans. Equity shares give the investor a stake in the ownership of the business. Preference shares can be participating (giving the investor a minimum annual dividend plus a share of the company's surplus profits) or convertible at a future date into equity. Similarly, loan stock can be converted into equity.

Secured bank loans are not venture capital, because the bank can try to obtain repayment from the sale of the secured assets should the business fail. Unlike bank loans, it is unusual for venture capital loans to be secured on the assets of the company or its owner/managers.

Categories of Venture Capital Investment

Business ventures for which finance could be required vary widely in character. But they can be categorized according to:

- industry or product
- size
- stage of business development.

Investments by Industry or Product

Investment risk varies by industry. High levels of business risk characterize some industries. For example in high-technology industries, such as computer hardware and software products, and medical and biotechnology products, companies rely on research and development to produce a successful breakthrough product. There is a risk that new high-tech products will not find a ready market, because of their price or serviceability, or will soon be out-of-date.

Some industries experience severe downturns and sharp upturns in their business cycle. Companies in such cyclical businesses as construction, normally enjoy large profits in the upturn and suffer sharp falls in profits in the downturn. Other industries are less cyclical and less risky, for example retailing and food production.

Size of Investments

Venture capital financings can be distinguished by the size of the investment. The smallest investments are normally in start-up ventures, and the largest in buyouts of major companies. There were several buyouts and buy-ins of major companies during the 1980s and 1990s that required funding in excess of $500 million.

Companies needing less than $100,000 or even $250,000 often have difficulty finding venture capital investors. The size of investment is too small to justify the resources (management time, etc.) of a venture-capital organization. Therefore financing must be obtained, if possible, from another source, such as a wealthy individual, or a big brother in the trade.

Investments by Stage of Business Development

Venture capital investments can also be categorized according to the stage of development they have reached when risk capital funding is required. These are shown in the diagram below.

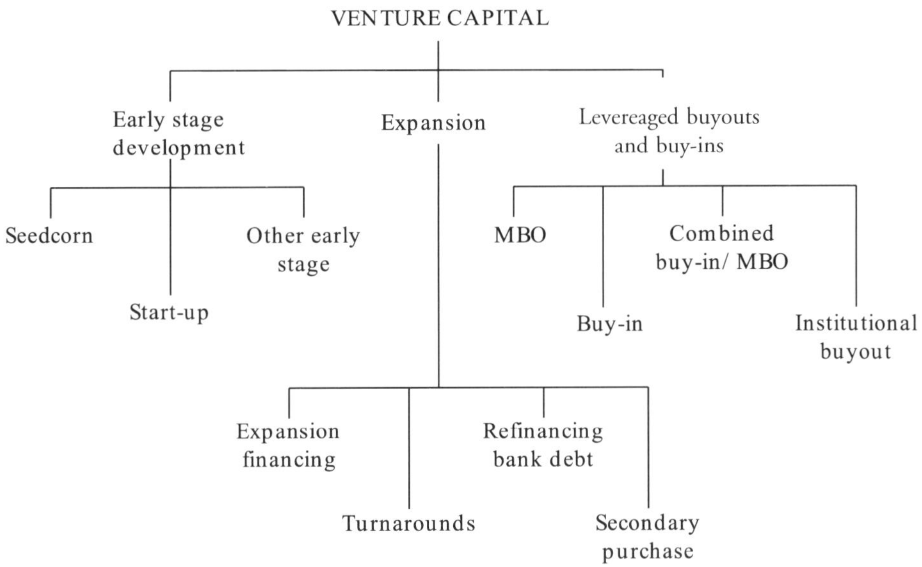

Seed Capital

Before a product-based business can be set up, there could be a lengthy period of research and development (R&D) to convert the business concept into a product. Finance, seed capital, can be provided for the R&D project. The developers of the concept, who might be research scientists at a university, could require finance to make a prototype, or carry out initial market research. The entrepreneurs themselves might finance an early phase of R&D. Seed capital, however, could be required to cover the costs of the prototype or the initial marketing in the period up to product launch.

Investing seed capital is a very high-risk venture. Potential risks include:

- a short product life cycle
- lack of awareness of competition
- launching the product too soon, before there is market acceptance
- launching the product too late, after a competitor
- inability to make the product work
- poaching of key technical staff by a rival
- lack of financial controls.

Start-Up

Financing could be provided to a company in the process of setting up, or at a stage where its product or service has not yet been sold commercially. The product or service exists, and in contrast to a seedcorn business, no R&D expenditure is needed before the company becomes operational.

Conventional wisdom is that for every ten start-ups, two will fail within two or three years and another two within five years. Of the remaining six, one will become a big success, one a moderate success and four (the living dead) will survive making only small profits and a negligible return for investors.

Other Early Stage Projects

Companies that have completed product development and begun marketing might want more funds to manufacture and sell the product on a commercial scale. These companies will not yet be making a profit, and cannot finance their development out of operational cash flows. Therefore they must rely on external funding.

Expansion Financing

Finance could be required for the growth and expansion of an established business. For example a company might wish to increase its manufacturing capacity, develop its marketing channels or invest more in working capital. Expansion financing is usually low-risk venture capital, compared with early stage investments and turnarounds.

Turnarounds

A company that has been in decline might develop plans for halting the decline and staging a recovery. In the early stage of a recovery program, the original backers will have to provide the extra finance required. If the recovery appears successful, other venture capitalists could be willing to inject extra funds. Turnaround financing is comparatively rare.

Refinancing Bank Debt

An established company burdened by bank debts, possibly reaching maturity, might seek venture capital funding to repay the banks.

Secondary Purchase

In a secondary purchase, existing shares in a company are purchased by one venture capital firm from another, or from another shareholder or shareholders in the company. Although venture capital finance is being invested, it replaces existing capital and does not provide any additional capital to the company concerned.

Management Buyouts and Buy-Ins

A management buyout is the purchase of an existing company or a business unit by a group of its managers, with the support of external investors, typically from venture capital sources and bank loans.

By contrast, a management buy-in, (MBI), is the purchase of an existing company or a business unit by an external management team, with financing from venture capitalists and banks. The buy-in team must have the necessary experience and/or expertise to run the business they are purchasing.

A number of MBOs and MBIs are of companies, or parts of companies, that have gone into receivership, where the business is in danger of disappearing altogether. In these situations, venture capital helps preserve businesses and jobs.

Management buyouts and buy-ins attract most of the venture capital finance that is invested because generally they are much bigger than other types of venture. Buyouts and buy-ins are the subject of Chapter 3.

Initial and Subsequent Financings

Companies that receive venture capital finance often will require further finance as they develop, or as they undergo further changes. A distinction is made between

- new investment, when a venture capital organization provides funds to a company for the first time, and
- follow-on investment, when the same venture capitalist makes a further investment at a later time in the same company.

The agreement to make a follow-on investment could have been reached in principle when the original investment was made, as a requirement for the planned expansion of the business.

A successful company is not obliged to use the same venture capital organizations each time it needs new finance. Second-round financing can be sought by a successful business, e.g. a buyout, from either its original backers or from a different investor group.

When a company is unsuccessful initially, its management could seek second-round financing from its original backers to continue in business. The backers might agree to provide extra financing, but insisting on management changes as a condition of their support.

Third-round financing could be sought by a successful company planning a major expansion program. At this stage the company might be in a position to obtain a stock market listing, and no longer need venture capital.

Venture capitalists holding shares in the company could then use the opportunity to sell their shares and realize their investment. Alternatively, further expansion capital might be sought from the original backers.

According to the Center for Management Buy-Out Research, US venture capitalists invest much more in early stage ventures than most others, while expansion investments are more popular.

In 1996 US venture firms invested more than $10 billion, $2.3 billion in the first quarter of 1997, and $3.18 billion in the second quarter of 1997.

In the Netherlands and France, expansion finance forms the largest single investment stage. In the UK, investment in MBOs represents nearly 65% of all investments; however, in continental Europe the average value of investments in MBOs has tended historically to be very small.

Venture Capital Investments by Industry, Second Quarter 1997

Industry	Investment ammount	% of Total
Biotechnology	150,121,000	4.7%
Business Services	125,828,000	4.0%
Communications	702,408,000	22.1%
Computers and Peripherals	195,121,000	6.1%
Consumer	173,285,000	5.4%
Distribution/Retailing	165,060,000	5.2%
Electronics and Instrumentation	63,213,000	2.0%
Environmental	23,848,000	0.7%
Healthcare	265,078,000	8.3%
Industrial	123,723,500	3.9%
Medical Instruments	165,186,000	5.2%
Miscellaneous	50,000	0.0%
Pharmaceuticals	97,327,000	3.1%
Semiconductors/Equipment	19,850,000	0.6%
Software and Information	910,618,000	28.7%
Total	$3,180,716,500	100.0%

Source: Price Waterhouse

Angel Investors vs. Venture Capital Funds, 1996

Angel Investors 1996	
Number of angel Investors	250,000
Number of Investments annually	30,000–40,000
Annual investment	$10 billion–$20 billion
Average equity share	20% (ranges from 10%–40%)
Average investment size	$300,000–$500,000
Largest investment	$1 million
Length of investment	5–10 years
Average return on investment	25%–40%
Percentage of funds invested in start-ups	90%–100%
Hottest target industry	technology (internet technology, new technology, technology applications)

Venture Capital Funds, 1996	
Number of venture funds	300–400
Number of investments annually	1,000
Annual investment	more than $10 billion
Average equity share in start-ups	41%
Average investment size	$3 million–$7 million
Length of investment	3–7 years (5 is most typical)
Largest investment	$110 million
Average return on investment	28%–40%
Percentage of funds invested in start-ups	10%
Hottest target industry	Communications, healthcare

Sources: Centre for Venture Research; National Venture Capital Association; Venture One Corporation

Conclusion

Venture capital is risk capital provided to private companies. It can vary from small amounts for start-up businesses or small companies to large amounts (sometimes several hundred million pounds) for management buyouts or management buy-ins of large divisions of public companies.

A venture capitalist shares both the risks and rewards of the entrepreneurial owners of the business, who are normally also its senior managers. Further finance can be provided, after the initial investment, to help sustain growth.

There is a key difference between borrowed money and venture capital. Banks receive interest on loans and expect the debt principal to be repaid according to an agreed schedule. If the borrower defaults, the bank can take action to recover the outstanding debts, and could decide to force the borrowerís business into liquidation. Venture capital, in contrast, is risk capital. Venture capitalists consider themselves as partners of the owner/managers, expecting to share in the success of the business through dividends or capital gains on their equity investments.

Venture capital can be a vital source of finance to small but growing businesses. A problem, however, is to find

- investors willing to put money into high risk ventures, and
- a means of channeling venture capital funds into companies that need the money.

Raising venture capital and matching investors with companies is a function of the venture capital industry that is now well established worldwide.

The Venture Capital Industry

The origins of the venture capitalist can be traced back to merchant venturers in the 15th century, when expeditions by Europeans to countries such as India, Japan and the East Indies were financed by wealthy individuals, who risked capital on the success of the enterprise.

A venture capital industry began to develop in the US in the late 1950s, but the foundations of venture capital for industry date back to the UK in the late 18th century, when entrepreneurs of the industrial revolution such as Brunel, Crompton and Stephenson, obtained financial backing from wealthy individuals to finance their projects.

The huge expansion in the industry worldwide has occurred much more recently, and dates back to the early 1980s.

Venture Capital Organizations

Although venture capital is sometimes provided by individuals and by investment institutions, the main providers are clearly specialist venture capital organizations.

A key feature of the venture capital industry is the bridge that it creates between investors and companies, i.e. between supply and demand for risk capital.

There are five broad types of venture capital organization:

- independents
- captives

- semi-captives
- government departments or agencies
- venture capital trusts.

They differ in how they raise funds to invest in ventures, and who controls their investment decisions.

Independents

Independent venture capital organizations raise their funds from more than one source, mainly institutional investors. No single shareholder or investor has a dominant position in the ownership of the fund. The funds are managed independently, and management is free to choose how the money should be invested.

Wholly independent funds can be set up in one of two ways.

- A group of experienced venture capitalists could seek backing from several investment institutions that put money into a fund that venture capitalists manage on their behalf.
- A group of financial institutions could agree to set up a fund, and recruit a management team to make the investments. The fund managers then decide how to invest the money in business ventures.

Investors in the funds are paid returns out of the proceeds from investing in business ventures, i.e. dividends on shares, interest on loans and the cash proceeds from the eventual sale or redemption of the investments.

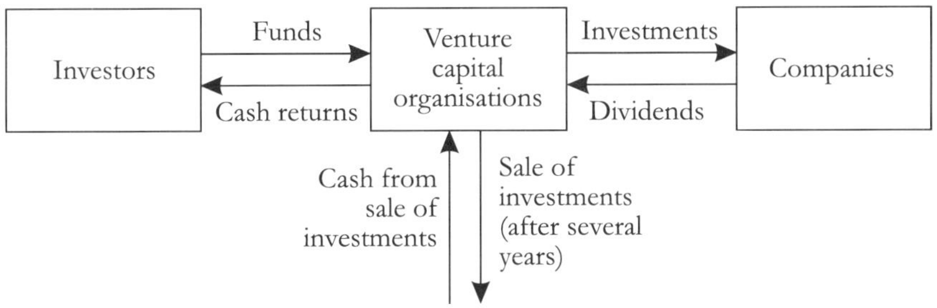

Independent funds have several other features.

- Usually they are close-ended, having a specified initial capital base. For example, a $20 million fund might be established. After the initial fund-raising, no further money will be sought for the fund, and management will invest in business ventures until all the money in the fund is used.
- Primarily they are equity-oriented, and seek long-term capital gain rather than a regular flow of annual dividend income.
- Often they are established with a maximum life, typically 10 years. At the end of this time, the fund is liquidated, and the proceeds distributed (in cash or as unsold securities owned by the fund) to the fund investors and managers in a pre-arranged proportion. Management can, if it wishes, set up a new fund to attract fresh venture capital.

Captives

A captive venture capital organization obtains its funds from a parent organization, usually a financial institution. The funds are managed on behalf of the parent organization. The management team is appointed by and is accountable to the parent that expects the fund to provide a suitable return.

Captive funds are often more concerned than independents about an annual running yield, i.e. dividend income, from their investments. Capital gain is nevertheless an important element of the overall return.

Semi-Captives

A semi-captive venture capital organization invests funds on behalf of a parent but also manages independently funds obtained from other sources. A merchant bank or other investment institution could set up a fund and appoint a management team, then invite a number of other investment institutions to join the fund.

Funding of Venture Capital Organisations

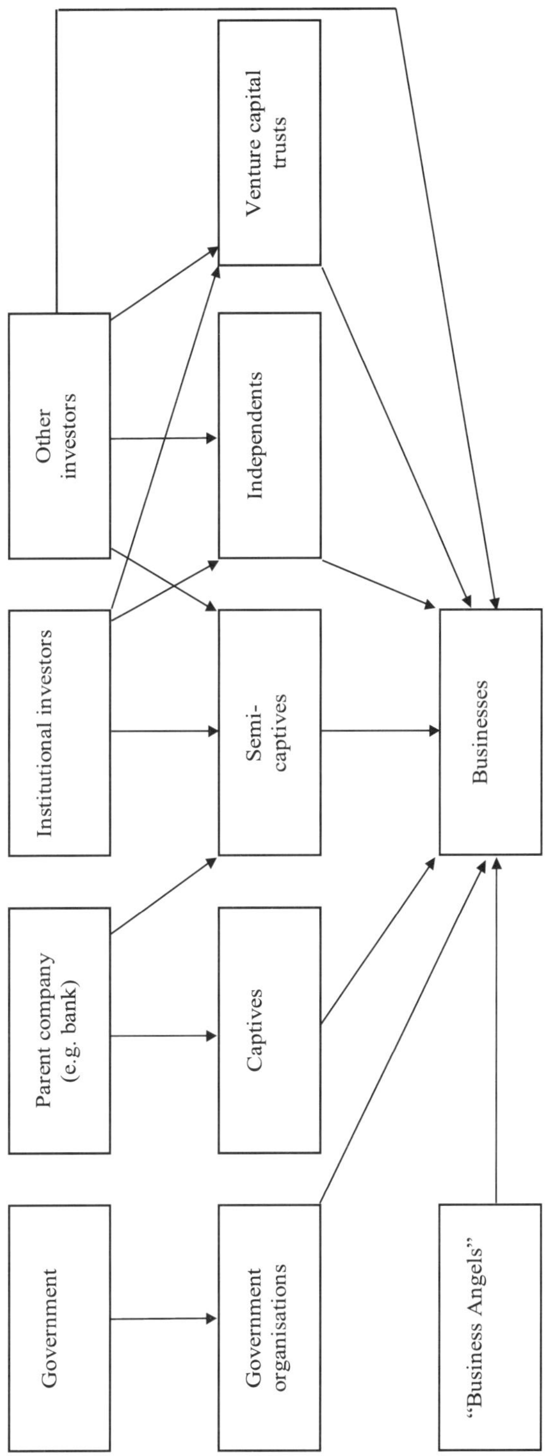

Advisory Services

Instead of investing funds under its management, a venture capitalist also could act as adviser to other fund managers or venture capital investors.

Size of the Venture Capital Industry

The venture capital industry has grown substantially since the early 1980s, in terms of the number of venture capital organizations, the amount of funds provided and the number of financings.

United States

The first US organization to provide risk capital for new and growing firms was American Research & Development, established in 1946. Venture capital funds have supported many US companies, for example Apple Computer, Compaq Computer, Digital Equipment Corporation and Sun Microsystems. The growth of the US personal computer industry is generally regarded as the main success story for venture capital investment in the past 20 years.

In the absence of major new technological discoveries, however, the investment emphasis has now switched from start-ups to more established businesses, particularly buyouts and buy-ins.

Europe and Japan

Within Europe the majority of venture capital investment has taken place in the UK, because of the strong tradition by continental family business owners of passing on their companies to family members rather than selling to management. However, privatization, corporate restructuring, changing attitudes to shareholder value among large corporates and problems ensuring family succession in private companies have all led to an increase in venture capital investment. At the same time, UK venture capitalists are more ready to look outside the UK to invest funds.

The continental venture capital industry has been growing rapidly. The European Venture Capital Association (EVCA) had only 43 founding members in 1983; by 1997 it had nearly 400, investing a record £6.8 billion in 1996. The number of transactions, however, is still at a very low level relative to the US and the UK.

By international standards, Japan is very short of venture capital. Japanese venture capital organizations prefer to invest what capital they have in development finance rather than start-ups.

The Size of Financings

The size of the financing that businesses require varies substantially. MBOs and management buy-ins generally require more capital than start-up or expansion schemes. In 1996, for example, venture capital financings of MBOs and MBIs represented about 33% of the total number of financings but about 74% of venture capital funds invested.

Venture capital finance is commonly provided as part of a larger financing package that includes bank loans or bond issues. During the late 1980s for example, there were many leveraged financings, in particular leveraged buyouts, where most of the finance was provided in the form of debt capital.

The amount of finance that a venture capital organization will commit to a single venture varies considerably. Some venture capitalists might be prepared to consider proposals for a minimum of $250,000. Occasionally, organizations might consider investing less, but these tend to be industry or regional specialists, and are the exception. Many organizations do not consider investments of less than $1 million because of the management resources required first to investigate each proposal and then to monitor the progress of each investment.

There is also a maximum amount that most venture capitalists are willing to risk in a venture. Organizations usually indicate a minimum and maximum preference for the size of their investments.

Syndicated Financings

Because venture capital is high-risk funding, organizations are often reluctant to become over-exposed to individual ventures. Although a venture capital provider could be willing to invest the full amount of all finance required for smaller ventures, usually it would prefer to share the risk in larger ventures with other venture capitalists.

Many larger deals are therefore syndicated financings, with several organizations contributing venture capital. One organization acts as a lead manager

- carrying out the initial valuation of the proposal from the entrepreneur/company management team
- assembling the venture capital syndicate and the financing package, and
- remaining the main point of contact with the company after finance has been provided; for example, nominating the venture capitalistsí representative on the company's board of directors.

Example

In September 1994 Nutreco was acquired in a management buyout from BP in a $550 million deal. Nutreco is one of the world's largest nutrition companies, whose businesses include aquaculture, agricultural specialists, breeding and feed and animal products.

The deal was jointly led and arranged by Cinven and Baring Capital Investors, who syndicated the equity provision to ABN AMRO, Commercial Union Asset Management, Foreign and Colonial Ventures, Montagu Private Equity, Ontario Teachers' Pension Plan Board, Prudential Venture Managers, SO. PA. F. International and Candover.

Debt facilities were also provided by Deutsche Morgan Grenfell and syndicated to a group of banks.

Another feature of the late 1990s was the establishment of tie-ups between venture capital firms, particularly cross-border, to enable them to source and negotiate deals more effectively. For example, in late 1997 Electra Fleming acquired FBG, a Hamburg-based private equity firm, and already had a 33% stake in an Italian joint venture.

Small Financings

A number of networks, called business angels, have developed that act as individuals or part of informal syndicates to provide smaller sums of finance at an earlier stage than are available from venture-capital firms. This capital may help to take the investee business to the point at which it may be attractive to a venture capital firm.

Term of Investments

Venture capital should be medium-to-long-term finance. Some venture capitalists have retained a long-term equity investment in companies they have financed. However, once a company has become successful, it should not have further need for venture capital. Venture capital finance, on which interest costs or returns to equity shareholders are high, should therefore be replaced by mainstream (lower-cost) investment finance.

Exit Routes

A venture capital organization will require an exit route for its investments. An exit route is a means by which the investment eventually can be sold for cash. There are five main exit routes, as shown in the diagram below.

The most common exit route is a trade sale to a buyer, usually another company in the same industry. The management of the company possibly could afford to buy the venture capitalist's shares, and preserve its independence. Alternatively a long-term investor could be found to buy the venture capitalists' shares (a refinancing).

Provided market sentiment permits at the time of exit, a stock market listing is available to companies that are large enough and have a suitable track record of profits.

Exit Routes

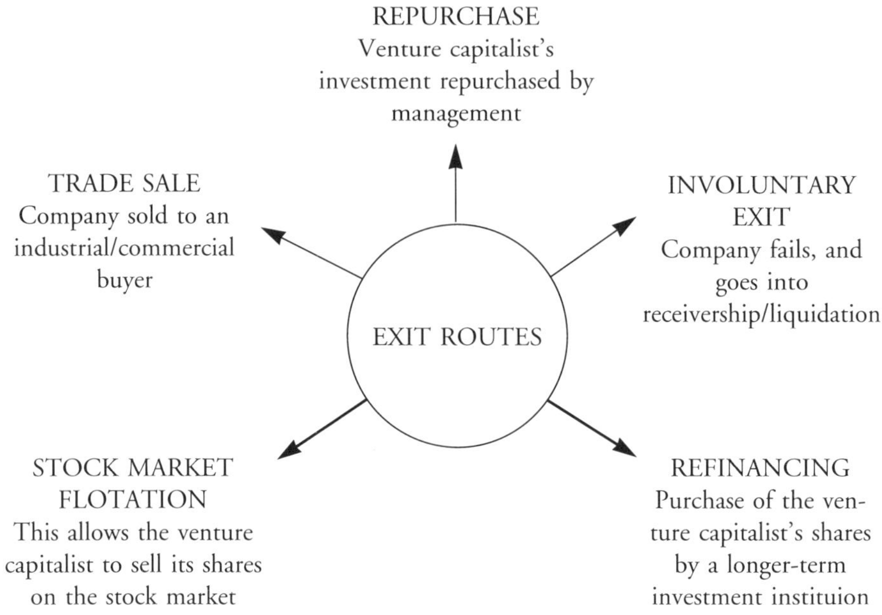

In 1997-1998, for example, flotations of venture capital-backed companies included chemical development company Oxford Assymetrics and IT company Guardian iT, both listed in London. In addition SELECT Software Tools was listed on NASDAQ and MobilCon became the first company to be listed on the Frankfurt Neuer Markt. Going public, however, has drawbacks as well as advantages.

The majority of exits take place by way of trade sale. Some venture capitalists have been criticized for wanting an exit route for their investments after only three or four years, and sometimes less. Often this does not give the company enough time to become successful and to provide the returns that the venture capitalist requires. An exit route after four to seven years would be more appropriate. In practice, the timeframe, from investment to exit, can be as little as two years or longer than ten years. For example, the Dr Solomon's anti-virus company obtained a flotation on EASDAQ in February 1997, less than a year after the original buyout.

Stock Market Listing

Advantages	Drawbacks
Owners can realize their investment by selling some/all their share	Loss of control to a wider group of shareholders
Stock market provides a ready source of finance for expansion, for example acquisitions	Possibility of hostile takeover bid
Enhanced status	Onerous disclosure requirements to meet stock exchange regulations
Opportunity for involving employees in share ownership (share option schemes)	Costs of obtaining and keeping a stock market listing
	Short-term view of stock market investors. Requirement for continual growth in profits, dividends and share price

Venture Capital Returns

Venture capital organizations are expected to earn satisfactory returns for their shareholders, parent organization or fund investors.

The continued existence of a venture capital market depends on the track record of successful ventures. Venture capitalists can tolerate individual business failures, but it is very important that on the whole, investment returns are high. Without high returns, investors will be reluctant to provide more capital, and the supply of funds will dry up.

The income of venture capitalists comes mainly from four sources

- dividends on share investments
- interest on loan/bond investments
- profits from the realization (sale) of investments
- fee income, including consultancy fees, arrangement fees, etc.

Losses are incurred when investments have to be written off or written down in value below their initial cost. The returns must be sufficient to compensate the venture capitalists for the risk. Returns from successful investments must cover losses on failed investments, and also provide a surplus to pay dividends to shareholders or make payments to fund investors.

Measuring Returns

Returns can be measured as an average annual yield on the initial cost of the investment that can be calculated by discounted cash flow arithmetic.

The return on an individual investment can be monitored at different times, from the initial decision to invest in the venture up to the eventual exit from the investment.

- When the business venture is first evaluated, the expected returns from financing the venture can be assessed.
- During the term of the investment, the returns consist of dividends/ interest received to date plus the increase (or minus the decrease) in the estimated current value of the investment, above its original cost. Often, ordinary dividends will not be paid in the early years.
- When the investment is eventually realized, the total returns consist of dividends/interest received plus the realized profit from the sale of the investment, that is its sale value minus the original investment cost.

Example

A venture capital organization invested $1 million in a company's equity shares for a five-year period. Dividends received were as follows:

Year	Dividend
	$
1	0
2	0
3	100,000
4	150,000
5	200,000

At the end of five years, the company's shares were floated on the New York Stock Exchange. The venture capitalist took the opportunity to sell its investment for $3,150,000.

Analysis

The pre-tax return from the investment is calculated as the internal rate of return (average annual yield) on the initial investment of $1 million. In this example, the return is about 30% per annum. This is shown in the table below.

Year	**Start of year**	**Required return at 30%**	**Dividend**	**End of year**
	(A)	(B) = 30% x A	(C)	(A) + (B) - (C)
	$	$	$	$
1	1,000,000	300,000	0	1,300,000
2	1,300,000	390,000	0	1,690,000
3	1,690,000	507,000	(100,000)	2,097,000
4	2,097,000	629,100	(150,000)	2,576,100
5	2,576,100	772,830	(200,000)	3,148,930

By the end of Year 5, allowing for dividends received in Years 3, 4 and 5, the venture capitalist would need to sell the shares in the company for $3,148,930. The actual sale value was virtually this amount ($3,150,000); therefore the return on the investment is almost 30% per annum over the five-year term.

Target Returns

In view of the high risk with business ventures, returns of 30% per annum or more are not unreasonable. A company seeking to raise venture capital finance should recognize the implications for its own profitability of having to pay such high returns to investors. Its expected profits should be large enough to provide the dividends and capital gains for equity investors to realize returns of this magnitude.

Investment Strategy

Each venture capital organization must formulate an investment strategy. An investment strategy serves two main purposes.

- It focuses management efforts and gives direction to the search for investment candidates. Without a focus, much time could be wasted on unsuitable investment proposals.
- For independent venture capital funds, an investment strategy helps potential investors to understand the type of venture their money will be invested in. Investors can then evaluate the risks and potential returns before making their investment decision.

The elements of an investment strategy should be:

- deciding which types of industry or business sector to invest in
- deciding on a preferred minimum and on maximum size of investment
- deciding the preferred stage/stages of business development
- deciding on a risk/return profile for the investment portfolio.

Industry or Business Sector Focus

Many venture capitalists are willing to consider investments in any industry or business sector. Some, however, are more specific about their preferences.

Some organizations will consider an investment in most business sectors, but refuse to invest in specific industries.

Some venture capitalists, while considering most business sectors, prefer to specialize as much as possible in one or two specific sectors.

There are several reasons for specializing in particular business sectors:

- the experience and expertise of investment executives. Venture capitalists employ investment executives with skills and experience in particular industries. Therefore they could develop a preference for investments in the industries that they understand best
- the policy of the venture capitalist's funds-provider. Government-funded organizations, for example, are likely to refuse investments

in industries that do not meet the government's criteria for new business developments
- some organizations either could avoid or seek to invest in high-risk industries. Some specialize in high-technology ventures, for example, whereas others rule them out.

Preferences for Size of Investment

Venture capital organizations set a minimum and maximum preferred size of investment.

The minimum size of investment should be determined by the cost of the resources (mainly management time) that are needed to evaluate a venture, arrange a financing package and monitor the venture's progress. The anticipated returns must justify the cost. This is why many organizations will not consider investments below $250,000.

The maximum size of investment usually will be guided by the total amount of funds available. For a small fund there is a risk in using the entire fund to invest in a small number of ventures. The failure of just a few ventures could jeopardize the overall returns from the fund. A venture capitalist should try to establish a wide range of investments in its portfolio so that the losses from any failures are always likely to be compensated by profits from the others.

Preferences for Stage of Business Development

Risks vary between individual ventures, but as a general rule, the greatest risk and uncertainty is during the early stages of a company's existence. Seedcorn ventures and start-up ventures have a relatively high failure rate. Established businesses, in contrast, are less likely to fail, particularly if the company has developed into a large organization with a well-established product range and customer base. Management buyouts of large companies should be comparatively low-risk ventures, provided that the financing of the venture does not create excessive financial risks through high leverage.

Some venture capital organizations specialize in comparatively high-risk or low-risk ventures. For most venture capitalists, investing in start-ups is either avoided altogether, because of the high risk involved, or restricted in the amount of funds at risk.

Start-ups are more likely to attract support if the risk is fairly low. It would be more willing to support experienced managers with a good idea who have identified existing businesses as potential acquisition targets to start up a new business.

Venture capitalists that are willing to invest in all stages of investment should seek a well-balanced portfolio, with investments suitably spread among different stages.

Risk and Return

The investment strategy of a venture capitalist should be to aim towards a portfolio of investments that provide a suitable balance between risk and return.

Each venture capital organization should have a reasonably clear view of

- the risks that it will accept in its investment portfolio, in terms of backing ventures in different business sectors, the size of investments (number of different ventures in the portfolio) and stages of business development, and
- the expected returns that it will require as a reward for taking on the risks.

Required rates of return will vary according to national markets. For example, an investor in a country with a high degree of political risk will require higher returns on his investment than one in a more stable, developed economy. Regional differences in inflation rates, interest rates and availability of investment funds and opportunities will also influence required returns.

Economic Conditions and Expected Returns

Anticipated returns will vary according to general economic conditions that affect all businesses. The returns on venture capital loans, both nominal returns and real returns, will depend on the general level of interest rates. Returns on equity investments are subject to variations in the business cycle. During a recession business activity drops and sales fall. Companies try to sustain profits by cutting costs. During an economic upturn, sales rise and prospects for strong profit growth improve. The expected returns from any venture over the next three-to-seven year period therefore will depend largely on the outlook for the economy as a whole.

Investment Opportunities and Expected Returns

The expected returns from business ventures vary according to the specific nature of each venture. Some businesses have better prospects than others, and are more likely to be successful.

The returns that venture capitalists can expect from investing in ventures therefore will be determined by

- the availability of ventures to invest in, i.e. alternative investment opportunities, and their expected returns
- the total amount of venture capital that is being sought by companies/managements
- the total amount of venture capital funds currently available, or that could be raised by establishing new funds.
- the degree of competition between venture capitalists to support ventures, or specific types of venture, such as management buyouts or media ventures, etc.

Financing Package and Expected Returns

The financing package for a business venture has to be structured in such a way that the business entrepreneurs or management team retain a significant equity stake in their company while at the same time allowing the venture capitalist to obtain a sizeable return if the company is eventually successful.

The Investment Portfolio

A venture capitalist's investment portfolio could consist predominantly of ventures that are very high risk, or of ventures with a comparatively lower level of risk.

An assessment of the risk in a portfolio can be illustrated on a two-dimensional map as shown below, where investment stage and business sector are shown as the two main risk factors. In the illustration, the portfolio is weighted towards lower risk ventures.

Protecting Investments

Venture capitalists usually will want to protect their investments by providing advice to management.

- By watching for any danger signals that could arise, problems can be avoided before they become too serious.
- By offering suggestions based on experience, the venture capitalist also can help a company make successful decisions regarding marketing strategy, product development, financial planning and management systems.

Venture capitalists should combine the financial skills of an investment institution with the industrial skills of business experts.

Risk and expected returns in a Venture Capital Investment Portfolio

	HIGHER RISK → LOWER RISK →					
		Seedcorn	Start-up	Expansion	Repurchase/ refinancing	MBO/MBI
	Medical/Biotechnical					X
	Construction					
	Computer hardware					
	Software					X
HIGHER RISK	Communication			X		
	Transport					
	Printing/publishing					X
	Electronics				X	
	Industrial products					
	Leisure		X	X		X
LOWER RISK	Consumer goods			XX	XX	X
	Food			XX		
	Consumer services		X			XX
	Retailing					
↓	Financial services		X			X

As a general rule, a venture capital organization is not concerned with the operational management of companies in which it invests. It assumes that the management team is competent and can carry out the business plan for the company. The venture capitalist will, however, usually require a seat on the board of directors. In a non-executive role, its appointed director can give general business and financial advice based on experience with other companies in similar situations, and act as the link between the company's management and their financial backer. For example, if a new business development is under consideration, the non-executive director can indicate the venture capitalist's probable reaction to a request for follow-on funds.

Therefore a distinction can be made between

- a hands-off investor (passive investor) who lets management get on with the job, and

- a hands-on investor (active investor) who encourages continual dialogue with the company's management.

The distinction is not altogether clear, however. Venture capitalists could regard themselves as hands-on if they insist on appointing a nominee to the company's board of directors. However, if the nominee director is not closely involved in the business, and takes a back seat, the investment is arguably hands-off.

Venture Capital Associations

In countries where the industry is now quite large, for example the US, UK and the Netherlands, venture capitalist organizations have formed a venture capital association. A primary function of such an association is to promote the venture capital industry by

- encouraging investors to supply funds and companies to apply for funding
- directing companies/managements towards the venture capital organizations that are most likely to be interested in their venture proposals.

A national venture capital association such as the National Venture Capital Association in the US, or an international body such as the National European Venture Capital Association, also functions to

- lobby the government on behalf of the small business entrepreneur, for example on matters affecting tax
- promote the industry by publishing information and performance statistics
- provide guidelines to members about the valuation of their investment portfolios
- promote education and training initiatives
- develop and encourage high standards of professional practise.

3

Buyouts

A buyout is the purchase of a controlling interest in a company from its owners. Any company acquisition is therefore a form of buyout. The term buyout is used more specifically to mean the acquisition of a business by a management team or group of employees with venture capital/bank support. Buyouts include

- management buyouts (MBOs)
- management buy-ins (MBIs)
- MBOs and buy-ins combined (Bimbos)
- institutional buyouts (IBOs)
- management buyouts.

A management buyout is the purchase of a company or business by a group of people who are its employees. An MBO can involve a single manager, but is usually a purchase by a small team of key executives, perhaps with more widespread support from many of the company's other employees.

MBOs of small companies are a natural phenomenon of business. During the 1980s and 1990s MBOs of larger companies and businesses were fairly common, with venture capital finance to support the management initiative. Conditions that must be fulfilled for an MBO to occur are:

- a willing seller
- willing buyers
- available finance, usually from venture capitalists and banks.

Reasons for Selling

For buyouts to occur, there has to be willing sellers. Business owners may be willing to sell for a variety of reasons.

- the owner of the business could be reaching retirement age, and wants to sell
- a parent company may wish to divest itself of an unwanted business that no longer fits in with its corporate strategy
- a company, having acquired another group of companies in a takeover, could want to resell unwanted parts of the group
- a parent company could decide that a part of its business is taking up more management time and group resources than it can justify
- a government organization could be willing to privatize some of its operations to raise money, for example the care of public buildings, or refuse collection
- the owners could need cash that they can obtain by selling the business. A parent company, for example, might want to raise money to pay off some outstanding debts and reduce its interest cost burden.
- a business could be unprofitable, and be closed down unless a buyer can be found
- when a company is insolvent, and goes into receivership or administration, the business could become available for sale, in whole or in part, to interested buyers.

Where management and employees join forces in arranging a buyout it is often referred to as a MeBo.

Management Buyers

The managers of a business often have ambitions to own it. They are in a good position to know when it could be for sale, and what it could be worth. This is particularly important in cases where a company is losing money, and would be closed down unless a buyer is found. It is possible that the management could see a way to turning round the fortunes of the business. The seller would avoid the costs of closure and the buyout team would have the opportunity to try to make the business profitable, saving jobs in the process.

Since the 1980s, it has been widely recognized by business owners that if they want to sell the business, the existing management could be a suitable candidate to buy it. From a financial viewpoint, it has also been recognized that if the management owns a substantial part of the business, it could perform much better than if the management were simply employees.

Providers of Finance

Except with small buyouts, the management team will need financial backing for their purchase, because the purchase price most likely would be beyond the reach of their private resources. Providers of finance are mainly venture capitalists, banks and occasionally, the seller.

Venture Capital Finance

Venture capital provides a crucial source of equity finance that makes MBOs possible. The financing package can be structured in such a way that the venture capitalist can expect to obtain a good return, and at the same time the management buyout team can own a large proportion of the equity.

Bank Finance

Buyouts of large companies/businesses cannot be financed entirely by venture capital. A venture capitalist will provide finance in the form of equity, preference shares and in some cases subordinated debt, but further financial support often will be required in the form of senior (secured) debt. Without bank lending support, MBO activity inevitably will be low.

Finance from the Seller (Vendor Finance)

The seller could contribute to either the equity finance or loan finance for a buyout. For example, a spin-off can occur when a business is owned by a larger organization that does not have the management or financial resources to develop it properly. The business is therefore sold off, except that the seller retains a minority equity stake. The spin-off is usually established as a new company, with senior management owning a large part of the equity.

A spin-off, with a retained equity stake, could be the preferred buyout option when the seller recognizes the potential for growth and profitability, but cannot devote enough time and money to make it a success. If the business does eventually succeed, the seller will make a gain on the investment, and could be well placed to buy back the company if its venture capital backers are looking to a trade sale as their exit route.

Instead of providing equity finance, a seller could provide loan capital, by deferring part of the purchase consideration. The unpaid part of the purchase price takes the form of a short-term loan. Deferred consideration is discussed more fully in Chapter 6.

Management Buy-Ins

A management buy-in is the purchase of a business by an outside management team. The buyers have no current connection with the business, and are not its employees. After the purchase they become the senior management responsible for running the company. A buy-in avoids the criticism of a buyout, that the existing management team has privileged access to information about the company.

Individuals in the buy-in team must have experience or specialist knowledge, to win the confidence and support of venture capital backers. Often a venture capital organization will build up a group of experienced managers willing to stage buy-ins, should suitable opportunities be identified by the venture capitalist.

Institutional Buyouts

During the late 1990s the institutional buy-out (IBO) became an established alternative to a trade sale for vendors alongside the more traditional MBO and MBI.

A typical IBO will come about when a vendor decides to sell a business in a controlled auction, offering equal information on the target to a limited number of potential buyers and seeking competitive bids for the company. Financial purchasers may enter this auction process on their own account, bidding against trade purchasers, other financial investors and possibly management buyout or buy-in teams. Incumbent or new management may be brought into the deals later, but generally will not be the initiators of the transaction.

Example
When Reed International put IPC, its consumer magazine publisher business, up for sale in late 1997, venture capital provider Cinven entered the auction process on its own account, alongside trade buyers such as Hachette, Time Warner and Bertelsmann. Of the 10 potential buyers' bids submitted, Cinven's offer of $1.4 billion was selected. Almost a third was equity and the rest was debt. A further $50 million was raised for working capital and expansion.

Buyout Activity

Provided that bank-lending support is available, buyout activity should remain high. After an economic downturn, when recovery is just under way, there could be several good opportunities for successful buyouts.

- Management could be attracted to a buyout because there will be early signs of an upturn in profits.
- Venture capitalists also would be attracted by the profit potential.
- Interest rates should be relatively low at the bottom of the economic cycle, and debt finance therefore more affordable.
- Banks could be attracted by the comparatively high lending margins they could obtain from loans to buyout companies.

Example 1
Succession problems among family shareholders led to the management buyout in 1997 of Edscha Group, a German supplier of parts to the automobile industry. A group of financial investors, led by PCA Parcom and advised by Palladion Partners, joined with management to acquire the share capital of Edscha in a deal worth DM150 million (approximately $82 million).

Example 2
In July 1997 the French utility company Cie Générale des Eaux sold its healthcare subsidiaries Générale de Santé and General Healthcare Group to their respective managements, for a total of $1.7 billion. The two buyouts were financed and negotiated separately but simultaneously advised by Rothschilds in Paris and London. The two deals were funded by $500 million in equity finance provided by Cinven and ABN AMRO, with debt finance provided by Bankers Trust and Société Générale. Cinven retained 80% of the equity on the UK side, the remainder owned jointly by the management and the equity underwriter. The French company had 40% of its equity retained by Cinven, 30% by ABN AMRO and 20% by Cie Générale des Eaux.

Buyouts of Quoted Companies

Buyouts usually involve the purchase of a private company or a business division of a larger company. Occasionally, however, there have been buyouts of entire quoted companies. The buyout of a quoted company can be an attractive proposition for the purchasers when the stock market has been in a bear phase. Share prices will be low, and provided they have touched bottom, the buyout team would expect to gain from a revival in the share price.

In recent years there has been an increase in the number of public-to-private deals, with management of smaller public companies becoming disillusioned with the stock market. For example, in 1998 the directors of B Elliott plc took the company private with a $70 million MBO backed by Deutsche Morgan Grenfell. Michael Frye, chief executive, said: "We are too small and complicated for the market. It takes them too long to understand us...." At the same time the management of Healthcall, another public company, launched an offer of approximately $80 million for the company, explaining that political sensitivities made it hard to run as a public company – there were too many conflicts between the demands of the market and those of its customers.

A controversial issue in buyouts is the privileged position of management, who could have access to information enabling it to judge a company's future prospects better than its shareholders. This situation is likely to occur in particular in the buyouts of quoted companies where shareholders do not have a detailed understanding of their company's affairs. The obvious suspicion is that management will try to buy the company for less than its fair value, although this is mitigated by the need for independent financial advice.

Example
An engineering company was faced by a hostile bid from rivals, but a white knight appeared in the form of an $80 million management buyout bid backed by venture. The hostile bidders attempted to discredit the MBO bid by highlighting discrepancies between a downbeat trading statement given by the engineering company at the time of its interim statement, and upbeat financial information given to its bankers shortly before this.

Buyouts and Investment Risk

A buyout involves the purchase of an established business. The commercial risks therefore should be known through the due diligence exercise. Investors also should be able to make a reasonable judgment about the company's prospects and scope for development and growth. The risks for an investor should, on the whole, be much less than with start-ups and early-stage ventures.

Even so, the venture capitalist is well aware of the potential investment risks with buyouts. An investment could be written off in full, written down in value, or yield very low returns.

Example 1
In 1998, a men's clothing retailer was sold by its parent company to an MBO team, but later the company went into administration. The CEO said that the company's problems were due to the reluctance of branded clothing manufacturers to sell through the chain that was perceived as having a very traditional image.

Small buyouts are less common than they were in the mid-to-late 1980s, but they require a disproportionate amount of time and attention from a venture capitalist backer. At the same time, access to bank loans is more difficult, and financing structures have to be more low-geared. For the venture capitalist, this means providing a bigger proportion of equity, and also taking on more of the risk.

It is therefore extremely important for the venture capitalist to have a strong management team in place, capable of developing the business and controlling costs. The potential rewards for backing a successful team then can be high.

Example 2
The Parker Pen company was purchased by its European managers, with the help of Schroder Ventures, for about $100 million in 1986. Management paid $1 million for 25% of the equity. The management team abandoned the unprofitable product lines, cut costs and improved marketing. The company was eventually purchased by Gillette, owners of the Papermate and Waterman brands, for around $450 million in 1993. The large return of the venture capital backers was dwarfed by the profits of the management buyers. The capital gain on the sale represented an annual return on their investment of about 300%.

Leveraged Buyouts (LBOs)

A distinction is sometimes made between

- a traditional buyout, where most of the equity is purchased by the management team, with a single financial backer, and

- large-scale buyouts, common in the late 1980s, where control is acquired by a syndicate of financial institutions and management has a relatively small equity stake.

In a leveraged buyout, a substantial part of the purchase is financed by debt capital in the form of bank loans, loans from venture capital organizations or corporate bonds. Many MBOs, MBIs and IBOs are leveraged buyouts.

During the late 1980s, UK buyouts typically involved a debt:equity-financing ratio of about 3 or 4:1. This contrasted with more highly leveraged deals in the US, where a typical debt:equity-funding ratio was 9 or 10:1. During this period, large-scale leveraged buyouts occasionally were the result of financial buccaneering by financial organizations seeking fee income from arranging transactions.

Typically, a company is set up as the vehicle for making the purchase. This is often a shell company that raises the purchase capital and uses the money to acquire the shares of the target company (or its assets).

Leveraged buyout

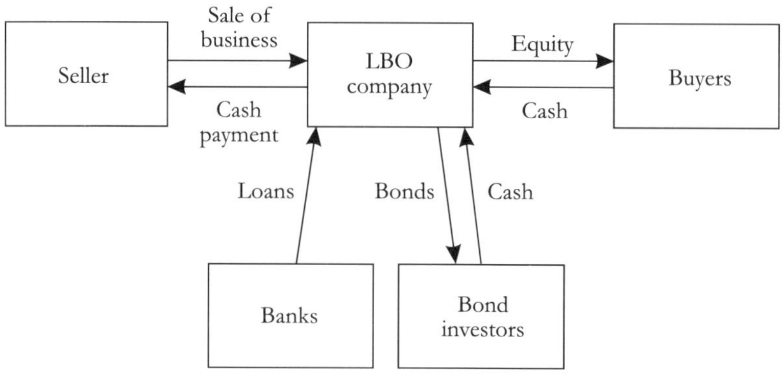

Example

UK supermarket chain Gateway, Britain's largest-ever leveraged buy-in, was bought for $3.6 billion in 1989 in a management buy-out engineered by US investment boutique Wasserstein Perella. Gateway was bought by a newly formed company named Isosceles, with Wasserstein Perella owning an initial 40% stake in the company.

Isosceles raised debt of over $1.8 billion for the acquisition. However, the combination of lower-than-expected cash flows, losses in a subsidiary and rising interest rates meant Gateway became unable to service its debt.

The debt was first refinanced in 1992, and again in July 1993. Under the second restructuring the mezzanine and senior debt lenders swapped $2 million of debt for equity, taking an 87% stake in Isosceles. The Gateway business was then transferred into a new company to manage the stores and assume £464 million in debt, with the remaining £923 million held by the parent company, Isosceles. As Isosceles itself had no independent cash flows, it proposed to repay its debt through the sale of Gateway that, renamed Somerfield, was listed in the UK in 1996.

A consequence of an LBO is that the bought-out company can be very highly leveraged. (LBOs are sometimes described as purchases that replace equity with debt.) The new company must be able to generate sufficient operating cash flows to meet its debt payment obligations. LBOs are viable only if the company is profitable from the beginning. The commercial risks with LBOs should be lower than for smaller MBOs, but the financial risks from the high leveraging could be exceptionally high.

In the late 1980s, a number of large LBOs were financed by junk bonds (unsecured high-yield bonds with a sub-investment grade credit rating) issued by the LBO company.

LBOs and Credit Risk

Because LBO companies generally are highly geared, there is a financial risk for both lenders and equity investors. A downturn in business activity, reducing cash inflows, could result in an inability to meet the company's debt repayment schedule.

Banks are reluctant to allow leverage levels of buyout companies to rise above 50% and typically will require cash interest cover of between two and three times on their lending.

Highly Leveraged Transactions (HLTs)

A highly leveraged transaction (HLT) is a term for any business acquisition that results in a highly geared business. HLTs include leveraged buyouts and acquisitions and recapitalizations. In 1989, three federal agencies (the Federal Reserve, the Office of the Controller of the Currency and the Federal Deposit Insurance Corporation) adopted the same definition of an HLT. To be classified as an HLT, a transaction should either

- result in a leverage ratio above 75%, or
- at least double the company's liabilities and also result in a leverage ratio above 50%.

The leverage ratio is defined for this purpose

$$\frac{\text{Total liabilities}}{\text{Total assets (including tangible assets)}} \quad \text{x} \quad 100\%$$

The government's concern about HLTs was the risk exposure of financial institutions that supported these transactions.

Conclusion

Buyouts are low-risk business investments compared to other ventures. However, the process of attracting venture capital support for buyouts is broadly similar to raising finance for other types of business venture. Venture capitalists require:

- a strong management team with a convincing business plan
- a secure and (preferably) thriving business (although buyouts could aim to turn around an ailing business)
- good opportunities for growth
- a fair price, so that a suitable financial package can be put in place.

The process of raising investment capital for all types of venture is considered in the following chapters.

4

The Investment Process

The venture capital investment process starts with the idea of an entrepreneur or management team that seeks venture capital finance. The role of the venture capitalist, having decided to support the entrepreneur, is to assemble a financing package leading to the launch of the venture. This chapter focuses on the buyout investment process. In essence, however, the process of obtaining venture capital is similar for all types of venture.

In broad terms, the stages for the entrepreneur/management team are

- identifying an opportunity
- assessing the price (for buyouts)
- drawing up a business plan
- obtaining financial backing
- structuring the financing package
- completing the deal
- second-stage financing (when required).

The entire process can be arranged within weeks but usually takes three to six months from initial discussions to completion. In extreme circumstances, when a business faces collapse, a buyout can be arranged within days.

A possible timetable for a buyout is suggested below. Throughout this period, the management team must continue to run the business.

Venture capital organizations search continually for suitable investment opportunities. Although specific investment proposals originate with the entrepreneur/management team, a venture capital organization can improve its prospects of finding investments by

Buyout timetable

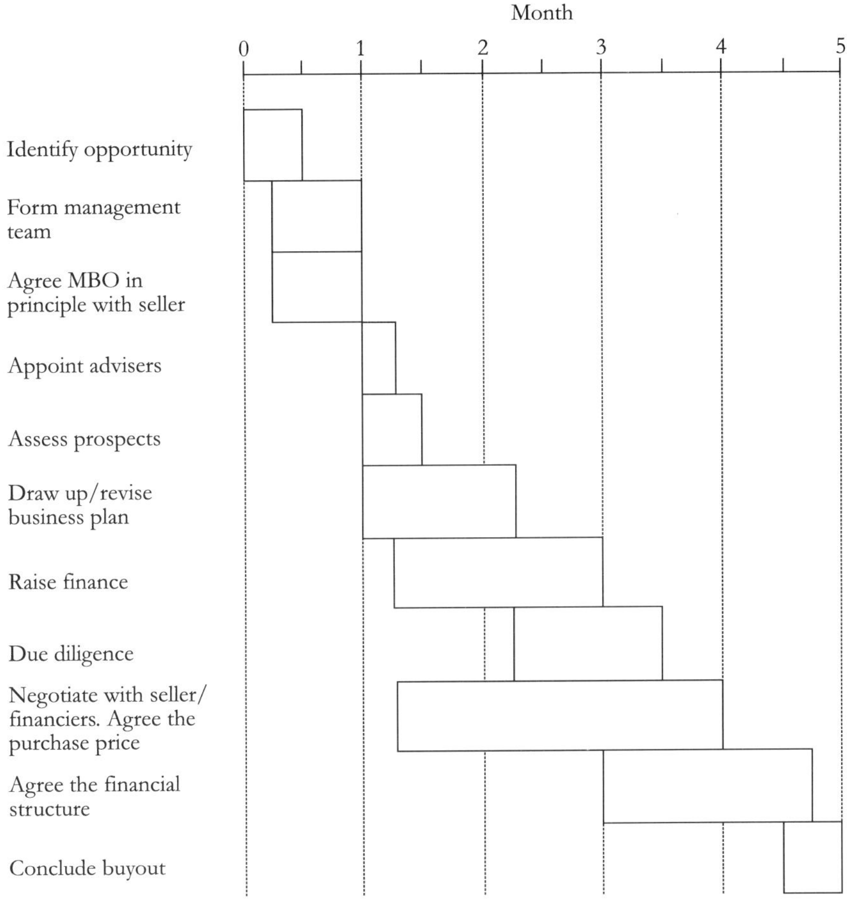

- publishing or advertising its willingness to consider providing venture capital, and
- identifying a group of individuals who would be willing, given a suitable opportunity, to become involved in a buy-in or buy-in/management buyout.

A shortage of suitable opportunities in the late 1990s has led to venture capital providers bidding directly to buyout companies, in competition with trade buyers and other financial investors. For example, the buyout of IPC , a European publishing company, from Reed International in December 1997 was an institutional rather than a management buyout, and was achieved in competition with a number of trade buyers. Also, in May 1998 UK venture capitalists CVC and Cinven made a successful joint offer of Fl3.4 billion (approximately $1 billion) to acquire Dutch packaging group Kappa Packaging from KNP BT, in an institutional buyout, beating a number of trade buyers as well as financial buyers Investcorp and Candover.

Identifying an Opportunity

The entrepreneur or management team who will run the business must first identify the venture opportunity.

In an expansion program or start-up, there could be a product breakthrough or a development in the market that gives a company the opportunity to make money, but only if it acts quickly, before anyone else. The answers to two linked questions should help the venture capitalist to assess how good the opportunity is and what the potential risks could be

- Why does the venture have to happen now?
- Why is the entrepreneur/management team better placed than others to exploit the opportunity?

Characteristics of a business that could make it either suitable or unsuitable are suggested below.

Characteristics of Buyout Opportunities

	Strong candidate	Weak candidate
Markets		
Established market		
Growing	√√√	
Static	√	
Declining		√√
New market		√
Products		
Established products		
Development potential	√√√	
Well established	√√	
Recently established	√	
Short life cycle		√
Declining		√√
New products		√√
Operational cash flows		
Strongly positive	√√√	
Moderately positive	√	
Just positive or negative		√√
Assets		
Sufficient for requirements	√	
Surplus assets (which can be sold)	√√	
Insufficient assets, need to buy more		√
Aging assets, need to replace		√√
Employees		
Workforce the right size	√√	
Larger workforce needed	√	
Redundancies planned		√
Management team		
Key group of 2-8 individuals	√√	
Key group of 10-20 individuals		√
Key individuals to be recruited		√√
Reasons for sale		
Not a core business	√	
Resale of unwanted business following an acquisition	√	
To raise cash to pay off debts	√	
Owners retiring	√	
Loss-making business; threat of closure		√

Products and Markets

Both management and their venture capital backers would prefer to have excellent prospects for making profits, but without excessive commercial risks. The most suitable buyout opportunity therefore would be a business with well-established products and markets, and with strong potential for further development. The company's products should have a large share of a substantial market or market niche. Products ideally should have a long life cycle, and there should be no foreseeable problems about finding new products to replace an existing, aging range.

Operational Cash Flows

Operational cash flows are an important factor. If a company's operational cash flows are negative, it will need additional funding to cover the deficits until positive cash flows are achieved. If the operational cash flows are small, the company will have very little scope for borrowing to meet its financing needs. The buyout company therefore should be capable of achieving strong positive net cash flows, after interest costs, as soon as possible.

Costs

With a buyout ideally there should be some scope for improving efficiency to reduce costs and enhance profits and cash flows after the buyout occurs. However, the same management will be in charge after a buyout as before. Thus there ought to be a good reason why the savings have not been achieved already. For example, certain practices or policies may have been imposed by the parent company, resulting in high overheads or uneconomic pricing.

Assets

The risks in a buyout are higher when there will have to be large capital expenditures to maintain or improve the operating capability of the business. In effect, a capital expenditure program would add to the total cost of the investment.

In an ideal situation, a buyout company should have marketable assets surplus to requirements that can be sold to pay off some of the financing loans for the venture, e.g. land and buildings.

Consequences of Going Alone

When evaluating a buyout, the management team should give some consideration to the potential advantages and disadvantages of breaking away from the parent company and becoming a stand-alone operation.

Advantages

Some of the advantages of breaking away from a large organization can be

- freedom from the bureaucracy of a large organization
- quicker decision-making
- avoiding the payment of management charges to head office.

Disadvantages

There could be significant drawbacks to breaking away from the parent organization that could affect the financial viability of the venture.

- The parent organization could be a major customer of the business. After a buyout, the ex-parent might be under no obligation to remain a customer.
- Other customers could be less willing to buy from a small independent company than a large well-established group.
- The buyout company will no longer receive centralized specialist services from head office, such as purchasing, treasury and tax planning, public relations, marketing and distribution.
- The buyout company will be less creditworthy than the parent organization. Credit terms from suppliers could be strict, forcing the company to pay for supplies earlier, and therefore having to invest more in working capital to finance stocks.
- Debt finance may be more difficult and more expensive to obtain.

The Management Team

It is impossible to understate the importance venture capitalists attach to the qualities and motivation of the management team or entrepreneur. In a buyout, the management team should possess, collectively, all the skills to run the business successfully. On the other hand, the senior team should be sufficiently small (eight at most) to be an effective decision-making unit.

The required skills, not surprisingly, include:

- experience in running a business
- technical expertise and knowledge of the industry
- marketing skills
- financial skills, these are particularly important.

A venture capitalist might agree to support a team with some missing skills, but would insist on either hands-on management by its own representative, or introducing someone from outside the company, to strengthen the team. A combined buy-in/MBO could therefore be suggested.

Example

A consortium of five organizations agrees plans to finance a start-up venture. The venture would cost $1.5 million and be all-equity financed. A small management team would be appointed to run the business, and the new CEO would be answerable to a board of directors consisting of one representative from each consortium member. Each consortium member, however, is only prepared to invest $200,000, leaving a $500,000 gap in the funding.

A venture capital organization is approached to provide financial support for the project. Anticipated returns are 50% to 60% per annum over a five-year period, based on what the consortium believes to be conservative estimates of market demand.

Analysis

The venture capital organization would probably refuse to support the venture at this stage. The venture capitalist would want to see an experienced management team already in place, with the key person(s) holding a substantial part of the equity.

If the venture capitalist liked the other aspects of the business proposition, it might suggest that the consortium should return at a future date with a management team, if the business were to require second-stage financing.

At this stage, a management team wishing to arrange a buyout should have obtained an agreement in principle from the business owner to sell. If possible, there should be some indication of what price would be acceptable. If the business has already attracted interest from an external bidder, the management team could be aware of what price or prices have been offered, and how the business owner has responded to such bids.

Assessing the Price (Buyouts)

With start-ups and business development ventures, the amount of financing required can be estimated from cash flow projections in the business plan. With a buyout, however, the management team has to establish a realistic price that the seller will accept but that will be financially acceptable to themselves and a venture capital backer. Establishing the price is a key issue, because it determines

- how much financing will be required, and
- the size of the expected returns.

It is advisable to establish a range of possible prices for a buyout by making three price estimates, a lowest price, a highest price and a realistic price. If the buyout seems financially attractive even at the highest price, the chances of success could be very good. If the buyout is unattractive at the highest price but attractive at the lowest price, negotiations on price with the seller will be critical in reaching a buyout agreement.

Having estimated a price, the management team should assess its requirement for equity finance (defined as common share capital and preferred share capital). This assessment will be approximate, but it should give the team some indication as to whether a venture capitalist could be willing to invest and, if so, for how much equity in the buyout company.

Example

A management team wishes to buy the assets of its business from the parent company, and expects the purchase price to be a maximum of $16 million.

The current assets of the business have been established as follows:

	$m
Land and buildings	7.0
Plant, equipment	4.0
Other fixed assets	3.0
	14.0
Stocks	3.0
Debtors	3.0
Total assets	20.0

It is assumed that banks would be willing to provide secured loans up to 60% of the value of the land and buildings, 10% of the value of plant, equipment and other fixed assets, 20% of the value of stocks and 70% of the value of debtors. Interest would be 10% per annum.

In four years, the company is expected to earn profits of $4.76 million per annum before interest and tax, and tax will be 30% of profits after interest. It is assumed that a venture capitalist would want an exit after four years, when the value of the company's equity could be nine times annual earnings (profits after tax).

The management team has $500,000 of its own money to invest.

Analysis

An assessment of the financing structure should begin with how much debt finance could be obtained.

The company's borrowing potential would be:

	$m
Secured on land and buildings (60% of $7m)	4.2
Secured on plant, equipment (10% of $4m)	0.4
Secured on other fixed assets (10% of $3m)	0.3
Secured on stocks (20% of $3m)	0.6
Secured on debtors (70% of $3m)	2.1
Total secured borrowings	7.6

With a purchase price of $16m and secured borrowings of $7.6m, the company's equity must be $8.4m ($16m - $7.6m). Of this, the management team can contribute $500,000, and venture capital finance must be $7.9m.

The estimated value of the company after four years is calculated as follows:

	$m
Income before interest and tax	4.76
Interest (10% of $7.6m)	0.76
Income before tax	4.00
Tax (30%)	1.20
Income after tax (earnings)	2.80

The value of the company's equity, at nine times earnings, would be $25.2m ($2.8m x 9).

The management team could estimate how much of this equity value will be required by the venture capitalist, in order to give a suitable return on equity. For simplicity, it will be assumed that no dividends will be paid by the company, and the entire return on equity investment will come from the proceeds of a trade sale after four years.

If the venture capitalist required a 30% return per annum, an initial investment of $1 would need to increase to $2.8561 ($1 x 1.30^4) after four years. An investment of $7.9m would need to increase in value to $22.56m ($7.9m x 2.8566).

This is about 90% of the estimated value of the company at the end of four years ($25.2m), leaving $2.64m (about 10%) as the return on the management team's own investment.

These calculations should help management to decide whether the financial structuring of the buyout, given the estimated price, could make the buyout financially attractive both to the venture capitalist and to the management.

Preparing a Business Plan

A business plan for the proposed venture is a critically important document. It provides a statement of what the entrepreneur/management team expects to achieve, and an assessment of the financial viability of the business. (The business plan is discussed in detail in the next chapter.)

Approaching a Financier

The business plan should already exist in a draft form when the initial approach is made to a prospective financier. The financier could be either a venture capital organization or a bank.

Venture capital organizations welcome the opportunity to assess proposals for business ventures, and use three methods of encouraging approaches from entrepreneurs

- referrals
- promoting their services (indirect marketing)
- searching actively for opportunities (direct marketing).

Referrals come from accountants, lawyers, bankers, businessmen and other venture capitalists, that introduce the entrepreneur/management team. Relationships are often well established between firms of accountants and lawyers and local venture capital organizations.

Venture capitalists also market their services in the financial press and at business exhibitions. Indirect marketing can encourage unsolicited approaches from entrepreneurs looking for a financial backer.

Direct marketing involves an active search for venture opportunities, through building up business contacts. Potential sellers and potential buyers can be identified with a view to arranging a buyout or buy-in.

A venture capitalist with funds to invest needs to attract a large number of potential entrepreneurs and buyout teams. Only a small proportion of the proposals received, perhaps just 1-2%, might reach completion. A rough guide to the stages at which proposals are rejected is shown below.

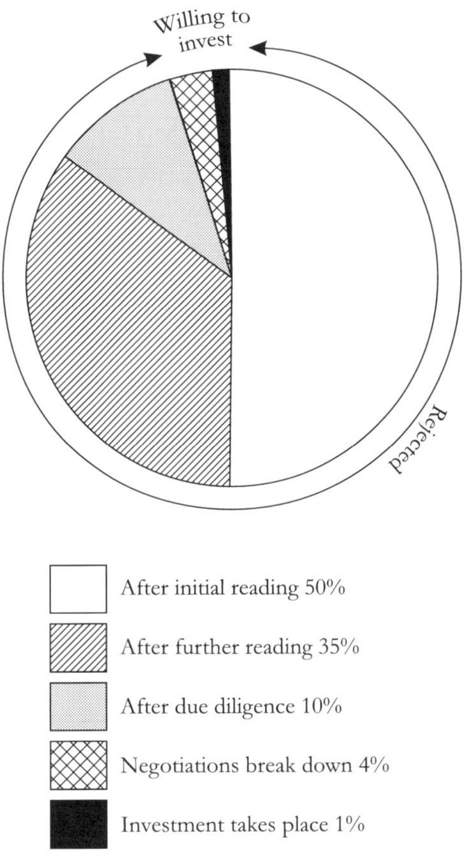

Negotiating a Financing

Negotiations between an entrepreneur/buyout team and a venture capitalist must go through several stages before reaching completion. The stages in the process, and the main documents that must be prepared, are shown below.

Stage in negotiating finance

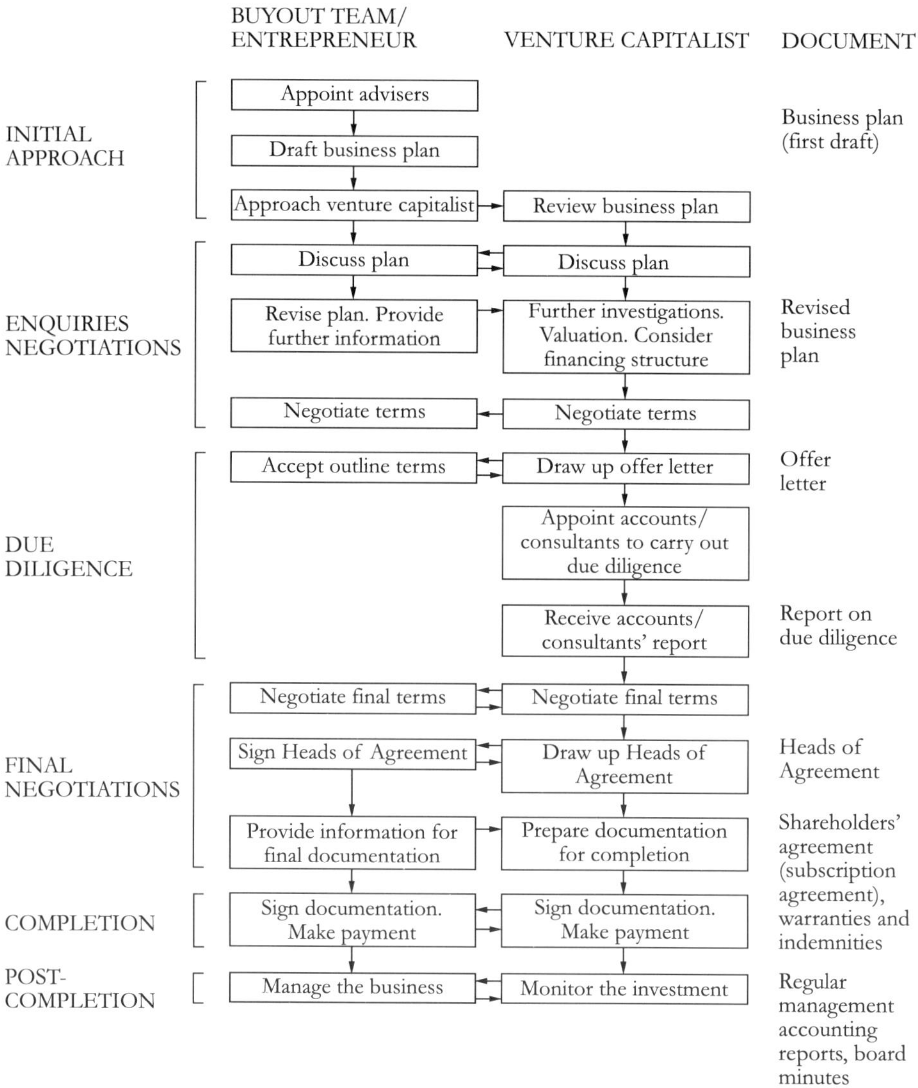

Initial Approach

When an entrepreneur/management team makes an initial approach to a venture capitalist, a draft business plan should be presented for assessment. The plan should be read by an expert with experience in the business sector.

The initial assessment by the sector expert will focus on the key basic issues of whether the venture could be a success, and whether the promised returns are big enough to justify the investment risk. A response should be given within a week. The answer could be either an immediate no, or a request for further information.

If the venture capitalist's business sector expert believes the proposal is worth further consideration, the financial aspects of the proposal will be studied by an accountant.

Risk, Return and Price

A venture capitalist will assess a business plan on the basis of the risk involved, i.e. the risk of losing the investment, the expected returns and the price (cost of the investment).

The risk in a venture is primarily the commercial risk that it will not be profitable, or will earn disappointing profits. In a leveraged buyout, however, there could also be the financial risk of high gearing, that the business will be unable to cover the costs of servicing its debts out of operational cash flows.

The returns from a venture can be judged from the financial projections in the business plan, to which sensitivity analysis can be applied. Major areas of uncertainty are typically

- the strength of customer demand, and the price customers are prepared to pay
- the time required for the market to develop (new products)
- the cost structure of the business. Costs can be particularly difficult to estimate for a start-up venture.

In the case of start-ups, a venture capitalist could expect to see, in appendices to the business plan, an independent market research study, an engineering study and a cost accounting study.

The risks and returns will determine whether the venture capitalist is willing to consider an investment, and the maximum investment or buyout price that could be paid, to provide a suitable level of return. As indicated in an earlier chapter, the expected returns from a business venture must usually be very high to win venture capital support.

Inquiries and Negotiations

During the inquiries and negotiations stage, the venture capitalist will get to know the entrepreneur/management team better. A meeting will be held to discuss details of the plan, during which the entrepreneur has the opportunity to sell the venture. At the same time the venture capitalist's investigating and negotiating team will be increasing its understanding of the venture, and re-evaluating its potential.

The entrepreneur/management team might submit a revised business plan on the basis of the new information they are asked to provide. The venture capitalist's experts also will consider what the business is worth, i.e. what its investment value should be, and formulate ideas for a financing structure. These will be discussed with the entrepreneur.

The methods used in valuing a business, and structuring a financial package, are described in Chapters 7 and 8.

During this stage of the negotiations, an outline agreement also should be reached on

- whether the venture capitalist will want to appoint one (or more) nominees to the company's board of directors
- the voting rights attached to the venture capitalist's equity shares and preference shares
- the level of warranties and indemnities that the directors of the company should provide to the venture capitalist.
- who will pay the costs of due diligence.

Due Diligence: Financial Checks

The Accuracy Of Financial Projections

- Have all costs been included?
- Have valid assumptions been used to forecast costs, revenues and cash flows?
- Are the forecasting techniques reliable?
- Does sensitivity analysis suggest a high exposure to some particular risks?
- Is the projected balance sheet of the business consistent with its current financial position (stock levels, debtors, fixed assets, investments)?
- Have management forecasts been accurate/reliable in the past?

Financial Risks

- Will the business have sufficiently strong cash flows?
- Will fixed assets be leased? What are the conditions attached to lease agreements?
- What are the existing bank facilities of the business?

Systems

- Does the business have financial reporting systems in place?
- Are the reporting systems sufficient to ensure good management control of the business?
- What will be the frequency and the content of management reports?

References

- References should be taken up on the business (from its bank, suppliers and customers).
- References should also be taken up on the entrepreneur/management team (previous employers, etc.).

Offer Letter

The venture capitalist will outline a proposed financing in an offer letter to the entrepreneur/management team. The offer is conditional on an agreement with the seller (in the case of a buyout) and is subject to the outcome of due diligence and other enquiries. The offer letter, when accepted by the entrepreneur, is not binding on either party. However, it is a statement of intent on the part of the venture capitalist.

Due Diligence

If a venture passes the initial screening test and an offer letter is sent, the venture capitalist will want to investigate the proposal in greater detail. Due diligence involves an investigation into the technical and financial details of the proposal. The purpose of due diligence is to identify weaknesses or problems in the proposed venture.

Technical Investigation

An investigation will be carried out by an external management consultancy firm, or by the venture capitalist's own experts in the business sector. Sometimes, where the target company is being sold through an auction process, the vendor may commission due diligence that is made available to purchasers. The aim of the investigation should be to establish the technical feasibility of the proposal, and whether the entrepreneur or management team has the background and skills to make the venture a success.

At the same time, the investigators will also look closely at the actual or potential market for the venture's products (or services), the nature of the competition, changes that could be happening in the market and any other factors that could affect the size and growth of the market.

Financial Investigation

Due diligence also involves a detailed investigation into the financial aspects of a proposed venture. The amount of available information differs between start-up ventures and buyouts or expansion programs. However, the main focus of investigation should be how realistic the figures in the business plan are. Issues to consider are suggested above.

Final Negotiations

Subject to satisfactory due diligence reports from the venture capitalist's investigators, external consultants or accountants, negotiations will continue to finalize the details of the agreement. The amount of investment required, the financial package, the venture capitalist's planned exit route and procedures for monitoring the investment must be agreed, and documented in a Heads of Agreement.

Appointing Advisors

A management buyout team or entrepreneur must usually rely on professional advice and assistance from accountants and lawyers.

Role of an Accountant

A firm of accountants, with experience in venture capital financings, should be appointed at an early stage. Accountants should carry out an initial assessment of the proposal, and if it seems viable, assist the management team/entrepreneur, if required, in the drawing up of the business plan.

The entrepreneur/management team could ask for continuing assistance until the deal is finalized, depending on their own financial expertise. Accountants could advise, for example, on the valuation/offer price for the buyout company, and the selection of a venture capitalist backer. Also

Tax Considerations

For individual managers	For the company
If managers raise loans to buy shares in an MBO/MBI company, interest on the loans could be allowable as tax relief for income tax Costs associated with a buyout may be allowable, either for the individual's income tax assessment or against future profits of the buyout company Managers are free to negotiate their own remuneration packages, subject to approval/consent of the venture capitalist. Tax benefits from various forms of remuneration may be available, for example a company pension scheme	Interest paid on loans raised by the new company to finance an MBO/MBI may be allowable for tax purposes When the MBO/MBI takes the form of purchasing the shares in a company, the tax history of the company is inherited. Any tax losses of the company before the buyout can be set off against future profits Warranties should be obtained from the seller of the company against any tax liabilities that might occur as a result of pre-buyout trading Capital allowances should be available (in the UK) on purchased assets, where an MBO/MBI involves the purchase of business assets rather than a company's shares

they could be asked to investigate the state of the accounts of the target business as negotiations for a buyout progress, and give advice on the tax implications of the venture, both for the business itself and for its individual owners.

Tax considerations are suggested in the table above.

Role of the Attorney

There must be at least two law firms in a venture capital financing, lawyers for the entrepreneurs and lawyers for the venture capitalist. In a buyout, the seller will also have legal representation. The legal roles in a venture capital financing are set out in the following table.

Role of Lawyers

For the venture capitalist	For the entrepreneur/management team
Draw up the offer letter, specifying in outline the terms of the financing	Check the offer letter and subsequently, the Heads of Agreement, and give advice on points of detail
Draw up the detailed subscription agreement (shareholders' agreement)	Negotiate the subscription agreement, and advise on the provision of warranties and indemnities
Obtain warranties and indemnities from the seller or company directors	When a new company is being established, draw up the memorandum and articles of association
Draw up any loan stock or debenture agreements	Negotiate loan documents on behalf of the client
Draw up the service agreements for key management personnel	Negotiate service agreements on behalf of the client
Draw up the Heads of Agreement for the financing	Advise the management team on the preparation of the disclosure letter from the seller
Obtain a disclosure letter from the seller. Disclosures in this letter can qualify any warranties given by the seller.	

Warranties and Indemnities

A warranty in a buyout agreement is an undertaking given by the seller to the buyout team or its financiers. If there is a breach of warranty, the purchaser can claim compensation against the seller. With an indemnity the beneficiary, e.g. the buy-out company, is entitled to full recompense from the seller for any loss on the occurrence of a certain event, without the need to prove the loss.

In a buyout, warranties usually cover the following broad areas

- the authority and capacity of the seller to sell the shares

- finance: a warranty could be given as to the accuracy of the latest audited accounts or management accounts, stock values and the level of provision for bad debts
- tax: it is essential to obtain a warranty that the company will not be subject to any unforeseen tax liability in the future, as a consequence of its operations up to the buyout date
- property and other assets: financiers will often want warranties as to the ownership of property and other assets used by the company
- future trading relationship with the seller: if the future of the buyout company depends on a continuing trading relationship with the seller, the seller should provide a warranty that this relationship will continue after the buyout.

Fees

Legal and accounting fees are usually payable whether a financing is successfully completed or not. Agreement on the payment of fees should be reached with the venture capitalist at an early stage in the financing discussions, and clarified by each client's accountant and attorney from the outset.

Conclusion

This section has described the venture capital investment process in broad detail. In the following sections, the business plan, business valuation, and agreeing the financial package for an investment will be considered in greater detail.

5

The Business Plan

A business plan is a document in which the management of a business or venture

- defines the business/venture
- sets targets for the future
- shows how the targets can be achieved.

It is the document that an entrepreneur or management team will use to persuade a venture capitalist or a bank to provide funds for the business. A business plan can be refined and improved during negotiations between the entrepreneur and venture capitalist. The initial version, however, must be sufficiently well prepared, to win the interest of the venture capitalist (and banks).

Although financial advisers could draw up a business plan, venture capitalists prefer the plan to be prepared by the entrepreneur himself, and most will provide guidance on contents.

Business Plan Contents

A business plan need not conform to a rigid format, but it should at least contain the elements shown in the table opposite.

The idea or opportunity on which the proposal has been based should be set out briefly in an executive summary at the start of the plan. The summary should explain the venture, why it will succeed, how much it will cost and what the returns should be.

Business plan contents

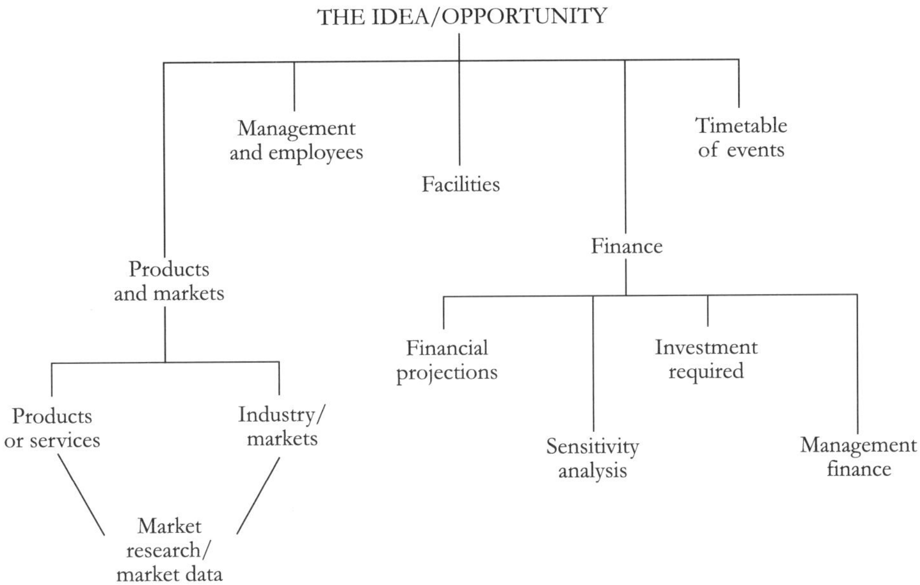

The Product or Service

The business plan should explain the nature of the product or service that the company intends to sell. The description of the product should give details of

- what it is, how it is used, who uses it, when and how often, and whether or not it is reusable
- its advantages over rival products, in terms of price, quality or the mix of price and quality
- its weaknesses or disadvantages compared with rival products
- its probable life span and the rate of technological change
- the current status of the product, is it in development stage, or a well-established product, etc.
- any patent rights or copyrights
- any industry standards or government regulations that must be met
- research and development policy and programs.

In the case of a start-up or expansion through new product development, the business plan will have to present a very convincing story about the uniqueness of the product and whether the technology exists to make it. In the case of a buyout, the business plan must explain why the product has a long-term future, or how obsolescence can be avoided.

The Industry/Market

A business plan should give a detailed account of the nature and size of the market for the company's products and the nature of the industry. A potential investor's main concerns should be whether the market is large enough and has good prospects for future growth, or, in the case of large MBOs, stability.

The plan should explain the particular segment or niche of the market in which the company specializes, in terms of product range, geographical area or type of customer. Precise details of the product and justification for the company's market specialization also should be given.

The business plan should also provide clear details of the competition, and in particular

- the number of competitors
- the identity of the main competitors, and the estimated market share held by each
- the strengths and weaknesses of the business compared to the competition
- how the company can successfully meet the competitive threat.

Marketing

A company must have clear ideas about how it will market its products and distribute them to customers. In the case of buyouts, marketing methods and distribution channels should already be well established, although there could be significant changes after the buyout. In the case of a start-up venture, a potential investor's concerns will be not just whether a market will exist for the product at the planned price, but also how the company expects to attract customer attention and then how it intends to sell and distribute the product.

Some of the key marketing issues are set out below.

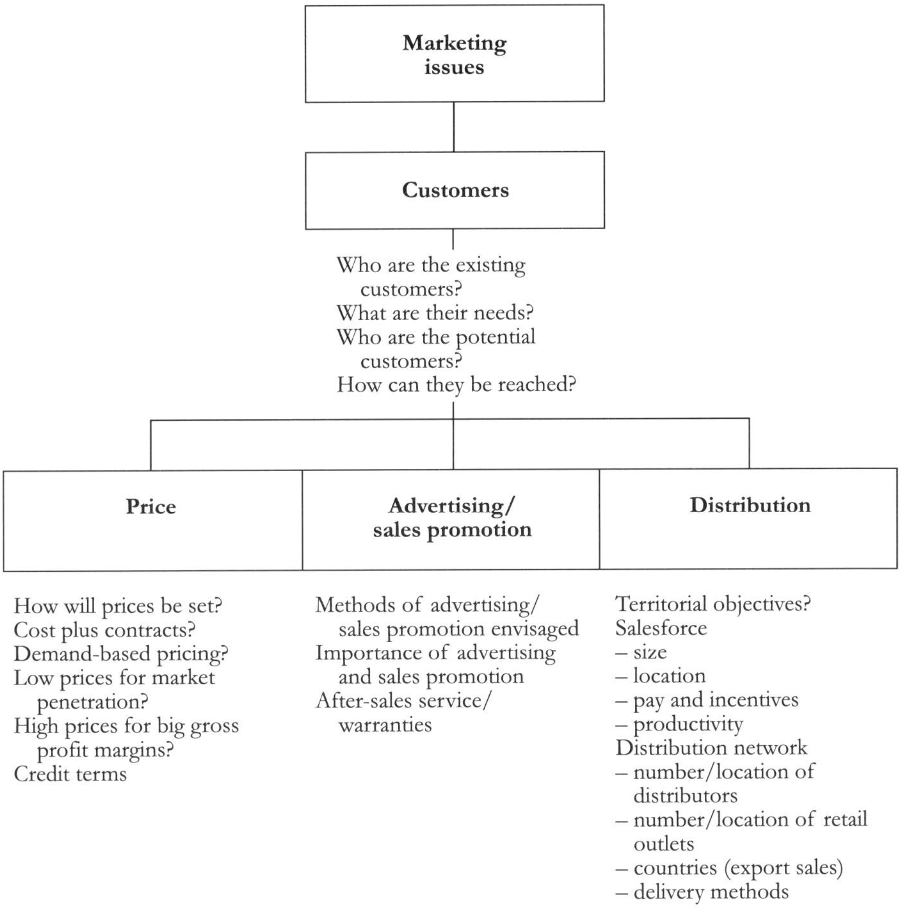

Market Research

Whenever possible, historical sales data should be used to prepare sales forecasts for the business plan. Established products of a buyout company have a track record of sales, from which projections for the future can be made. Assumptions must be made, however, about future growth or decline in the market. In the case of a start-up, assumptions are needed about the potential size of the market for a product, at a given price.

For both start-ups and established businesses, the forecasts in the business plan should also be based, to a greater or lesser extent, on market research. A difficulty for the entrepreneur/management team is the cost of hiring a market research agency. A balance has to be found between incurring market research costs, that the individuals concerned must pay for themselves, and providing convincing evidence to a venture capitalist that a viable market will exist for the company's products.

Management and Employees

An often-repeated observation by venture capitalists is that they invest in people, not in projects, and that it's better to back good management with a bad product than bad management with a good product. In effect, in a business plan the management is asking venture capitalists to trust them with their money. The plan must therefore focus on the experience and the qualities of the management team.

The section of the business plan dealing with management and personnel should therefore identify the key members of the management team, providing details of their age, experience and particular talents. It is important to show the balance of the team, and why it is so large or so small. The venture capitalist will pay particular attention to the experience of the chief executive and finance director.

The business plan should be honest about any gaps in the senior management team, and explain how individuals could be recruited in the future to fill them.

Motivation will be a key issue. A venture capitalist will expect senior management to have a substantial equity stake in the business. Remuneration packages should not be excessive: it is inappropriate to pay individuals more than the business can safely afford. However, incentives through bonus schemes or equity option schemes should be acceptable.

The business plan should also give details of the rest of the work force, with respect to its size, location, roles and skills, pay levels, recruitment and training requirements, and equity participation (if any). Where appropriate, a history of industrial relations in the company also should be given.

Operations

There should be a section in the business plan explaining how the business will operate on a day-to-day basis. In the case of a manufacturing business, the plan should describe

- the production process
- existing facilities (premises, plant, equipment, etc.)
- the new facilities that will be required
- production capacity (current and planned), including details of how production capacity will be increased
- the sources of supply for materials, components and key services, the security of supply sources, and alternative sources of supply
- any options that exist to produce internally or buy-in
- quality control procedures and wastage and scrap rates
- the cost structure of the business (costs at different output volumes)
- the labor skills required and the availability of skilled labor
- plans, if any, to change the production process
- the advantages, if any, over the products and the production systems of competitors

Financial Projections

The financial projections in a business plan will be subjected to rigorous scrutiny before a venture capitalist will agree to provide financial backing. Summary figures should be included in the main part of the business plan, with detailed figures in appendices, covering a planning period of (typically) three to five years. The purpose of the financial projections should be to estimate:

- how much finance will be needed by the venture (including the purchase cost, in the case of buyouts and buy-ins)
- the annual revenues, costs and profits of the business
- the cash flows, allowing for any planned capital expenditures and working capital investment.

The projections can be made in a forecast profit and loss account and a forecast cash flow statement. It is also useful to prepare a projected balance sheet of the business, as at the start and the culmination of the planning period.

Assumptions in the Financial Projections

It is crucially important to specify the assumptions on which the financial projections have been based. There are two main reasons for this.

- The assumptions can be checked for reasonableness.
- Where some assumptions are questioned or challenged, they can be altered and a new set of figures produced. This is particularly valuable for risk analysis/sensitivity analysis.

A list of assumptions that might be required to produce financial projections is shown opposite

Financial Assumptions

Sales
Level and timing of demand
Price
Discounts
Domestic/export markets

Operating expenditures
Salaries, wages
Commissions
Cost of materials/components
Cost of services and administration
Advertising/sales promotion budget
Distribution costs/freight
R&D costs
Product returns/repairs (level, costs)
Training/recruitment

Fixed assets
Capital expenditures
Depreciation rates on fixed assets
Government grants, if any

Cash collection
Credit taken by customers
Bad debts

Cash payments
Stock levels
Work-in-progress levels
Credit taken from suppliers

Tax
Value added tax rates
Federal and state taxes
Timing of tax payments

Finance costs
Interest (rates and amount payable)
Dividends
Debt principal repayments
Leasing (amount of equipment leased, repayment terms, interest costs)

Profit and Loss Account Forecasts

For the purposes of a business plan, it is advisable to project profits or losses month-by-month over a period of at least one year (preferably two or three years) and annually thereafter. Monthly forecasts are particularly necessary where business is seasonal.

Estimates of sales revenue (units and revenue) are usually the starting point for a forecast. Turnover is simply the volume of sales multiplied by the sales price (excluding any taxes).

Costs can be more difficult to forecast, and care should be taken in making the assumptions on which cost estimates are based. If possible, a distinction should be made between

- variable costs, that is costs that vary with the volume of sales activity, and

- fixed costs, for which total spending does not vary with activity and a fixed spending amount can be budgeted.

Cash Flow Forecasts

Cash flow forecasts, like profit forecasts, should be prepared on a month-by-month basis for at least three years of the forecast period. In the case of an ongoing business, e.g. a buyout, the starting point for preparing a cash flow forecast should be the profit forecasts. Adjustments should then be made to convert revenue and cost figures to cash receipts and payments, by allowing for stockholding, credit taken from suppliers, credit allowed to customers, the timing of quarterly, six-monthly or annual payments, e.g. rent, rates, insurance, and capital expenditures.

Depreciation charges, as a non-cash expense, should be excluded from the cash flow forecasts.

A venture capitalist will be particularly interested in this forecast that should show

- how much finance the business will need (from equity or loans) to remain solvent
- when the business should expect to become self-sufficient, relying on its own internally generated cash flows to meet debt payment obligations and for further funding
- the strength of the cash flows, and the potential for financing growth, paying dividends to equity shareholders and repaying outstanding loans.

Sensitivity Analysis

The entrepreneurs or management team preparing the business plan should ideally construct a model for their profit and loss accounts and cash flow forecasts. A spreadsheet model would be appropriate, and the assumptions on which the financial projections are being made can be written into the formulae in the model. The venture capitalist organization will also develop its own model based on the business plan, if it is interested in a detailed investigation of the project.

The main purposes of constructing a model are to

- simplify the process of revising the forecasts, should any assumptions be altered, and
- carry out sensitivity analysis.

The purpose of sensitivity analysis is to establish whether the financial projections would be significantly different if any of the assumptions changed. It consists of asking what if questions. For example, sensitivity analysis can predict what would happen to the financial forecasts if the market for the product were smaller than forecast, or if market demand took longer to pick up. Assumptions relating to revenues, costs, the timing of receipts or payments, capital expenditures and interest rates can all be altered.

The profitability and cash flows of a venture are likely to be unaffected by fairly large variations in some of the assumptions in the plan, but significantly affected by relatively small variations in other assumptions. For example, a project might continue to offer high returns if market demand were 20% lower, but would offer significantly lower returns over the planning period if the project were delayed by 12 months due to R&D and production hold-ups.

Sensitivity analysis can be used to

- identify key factors that will significantly affect the returns from a venture, and
- measure the extent to which the assumptions about these key factors must alter before the project ceases to provide the satisfactory returns.

Required Investment

The business plan should provide an estimate of how much funding is required. In the case of a start-up, the total funding will be:

	$
Costs of setting up the business (capital expenditures, etc.)	A
Working capital requirements	B
Finance to cover operating deficits in the early period of the venture	C
Contingency funds	D
	A + B + C + D
Less money invested by entrepreneur	- E
Finance required from venture capitalists/banks	A + B + C + D - E

In the case of an MBO, the total funding will be:

	£
Purchase cost of the business	A
Further capital expenditure (if any)	B
Additional working capital required (if any)	C
Contingency funds	D
	A + B + C + D
Less money invested by management team	- E
Finance required from venture capitalists/banks	A + B + C + D - E

If the management team plan to sell off unwanted assets after a buyout, or hope to reduce the investment in working capital, some of the required finance will be temporary and could be met by short-term bank facilities.

The purchase price for a buyout can be the make-or-break issue in negotiations between the management team and the seller, or the management team and the venture capitalist. The seller will often want to extract a high price, whereas the venture capitalist will be reluctant to pay an excessive price that will reduce the venture's expected returns.

The purchase price will depend on trading conditions at the time of the buyout. If the company is enjoying high levels of profits, and has a good trading outlook, the seller can demand a high price. If, however, the company has suffered a downturn in trading, and it is not yet clear that recovery is under way, the buyers should be able to negotiate a commensurate price.

Stages of Investment

The business plan should indicate the longer-term strategy for the business. If a significant expansion is planned that will require additional funding, the plan should provide an estimate of when the expansion is likely to occur and what level of funding might be required.

The business plan should also give some consideration to the exit route for the venture capitalist, indicating how the investment could be realized after a number of years, i.e. as at the end of the business plan period.

Timetable of Events

A timetable should be specified in the business plan, showing when particular events must occur for the plan to remain on schedule. The timetable should identify target dates for key events in establishing the business, such as the acquisition of premises, capital expenditures, the completion of product development, the launch of a major marketing campaign, establishing a distribution network, or reaching the date that the product/service is available for distribution.

Conclusion

The main purpose of the business plan is to sell the proposal to the venture capitalist. It is the key document for assessing the viability of a venture, and provides a basis for deciding

- whether a venture deserves financial backing, and
- the financing package that will give the venture capitalist the required investment return.

6

Sources of Finance

Finance for a venture can be provided entirely in the form of common stock, but is more usually a mix of two or more of the following:

- common stock
- preferred stock
- deferred consideration (buyouts)
- senior debt
- subordinated debt
- junk bonds (US)
- mezzanine finance (UK).

The sources of finance are:

- the entrepreneur/management team
- a trade investor/partner
- the seller (buyouts)
- venture capitalists (including wealthy individuals)
- banks.

Common stock

Subscribers for common stock in a business venture are the entrepreneurs/management team, the venture capitalists and, occasionally, a trade investor or (in a buyout) the seller. Common stockholders are the main risk-takers in a venture. They are not entitled to any dividend until interest has been paid on borrowings and dividends have been paid on preferred stock. If the company goes into liquidation, other providers of finance rank ahead of common stockholders in the right to repayment of their investment from selling off the company's assets.

Sources of finance for Business Ventures

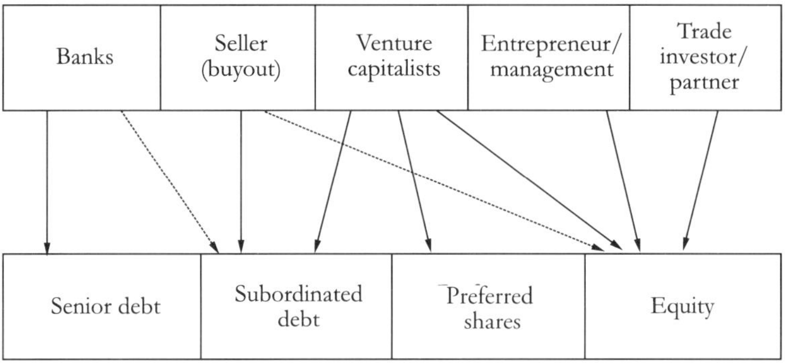

In return for taking the highest investment risk, common stockholders stand to earn the biggest rewards, and share in the company's profits after paying preferred dividends.

Common stockholders usually have the main voting rights at general meetings of the company, and management is accountable to them, as ultimate owners of the company.

In most companies, common stockholders are the owners of all the company's equity. In business ventures, however, there are often special rights attached to other stocks and loans, and the equity of the company therefore extends beyond the common stockholders.

When a business venture is established, the entrepreneur/management team usually will want to hold a reasonably large proportion of the common stock in spite of providing a much lower proportion of the total finance. For example, the entrepreneurs might provide 10% of the capital invested but receive perhaps 50% or more of the common stock.

The rest of the common stock usually is acquired by one or more venture capitalists. In some buyouts the seller could retain an equity stake, or another company could provide equity finance as a trade investor or trading partner for the management team.

Classes of Common stock

The venture capitalist is more concerned with returns on investment than with management control. Although entrepreneurs accept the need for the venture capitalist to share in the equity, they often want to retain voting control. An arrangement that can suit both parties is to create two classes of common stock. For example

- Class A stocks would be held by the entrepreneurs/managers, and carry most stockholder voting rights.
- Class B stocks or preferred common stock would carry fewer voting rights but a larger dividend entitlement, and would be held by the venture capitalist.

In negotiating a financing package for a venture, the venture capitalist might ask the entrepreneur/management team to give certain assurances about future dividend policy. This will reassure the venture capitalist that some returns will be earned, in the form of dividends, if the company proves to be profitable.

Preferred stock

A large part of the investment in a company by a venture capitalist can take the form of preferred stock capital. There are several reasons why preferred stock could be a suitable method of investment, relating mainly to control of the company, shareholder rights, and the risks and returns for the stockholders.

Preferred stockholders have limited control over their company. Management, that is ultimately accountable to its common stockholders, not the preferred stockholders, exercises control. However, preferred stock can carry special voting rights in particular circumstances or on particular issues.

Preferred stock can be more attractive to the company's entrepreneurs than debt capital because of the limited rights of stockholders in the event that the company is unable to pay a preference dividend. If the company is unable to pay a dividend, because of insufficient profits or cash, the preferred stockholders cannot take action against the company to obtain payment. This contrasts with providers of debt capital, who can take action for non-payment of interest or failure to repay debt principal.

Preferred stockholders are entitled to a dividend, providing them with a regular income. In addition, depending on their characteristics, the stocks also can entitle their holders to acquire common stock in the company, or to participate in the company's surplus profits. The potential rewards can compensate preferred stockholders for their investment risk, should the venture prove successful. For this reason, preferred stock capital is often regarded as equity by venture capitalists.

Preferred stock falls into one or more of the following four categories

- cumulative
- redeemable
- convertible
- participating.

Cumulative Preferred Stock

Unpaid dividends on cumulative preferred stock accumulate, and arrears of preferred dividend eventually must be paid before any dividend can be paid to ordinary stockholders. In contrast, unpaid dividends on non-cumulative preferred stock do not accumulate.

Example

A company has issued $1 million of 8% cumulative preferred stock of $1 each, on which dividend is payable in equal six-monthly installments each year. The company was unable to pay the preferred dividend in one year, but wishes to start paying dividends again mid-way through the following year.

Analysis

The company must pay the arrears of preferred dividend and the current preferred dividend before paying any dividend to common stockholders. If the company wants to pay an ordinary interim dividend in Year 2, the preferred dividend must be as follows:

	$
Arrears of dividend, previous year (8%)	80,000
Current six-monthly dividend (4%)	40,000
	120,000

Redeemable Preferred Stock

Redeemable preferred stock capital is repayable usually at par value, but sometimes at a premium above par value, at an agreed future date. In a business venture, the redemption date could be scheduled to coincide with the venture capital organization's planned exit from its investment in the company.

Convertible Preferred Stock

Convertible preferred stock can be exchanged for newly issued common stock in the company at an agreed future date, and at the option of the shareholder. The rate of conversion from preferred stock into common stock is fixed when the preferred stock is issued. Until converted, the stock carries an entitlement to an annual dividend.

Convertible preferred stock allows a venture capitalist to benefit from the success of the company, through conversion into common stock. The common stock can be sold to realize a profit when an exit for the investment is available. Until conversion, the stocks rank ahead of common stock in their entitlement to dividend. The option to convert into common stock should be scheduled to occur either before or at the venture capitalist's planned exit date.

Participating Preferred Stock

Participating preferred stock carries entitlement to a basic dividend plus a share in profits of the company above a certain level. The preferred stockholders therefore participate with common stockholders in the surplus profits of the business. They are sometimes described as participating preferred common stock.

The terms of participation vary, and are subject to negotiation when the financing package for the venture is assembled.

Example

A company has issued the following share capital

	$
Common stock of $1	500,000
Participating preferred stock of $1	2,000,000
	2,500,000

Preferred stockholders are entitled to a dividend of 10% each year, plus 25% of the post-tax profits of the company in excess of $800,000 per annum.

Analysis

Suppose the company's annual profits are $1,200,000. The preferred dividend will be as follows

	$
Basic dividend at 10%	200,000
25% of profits in excess of $800,000 (25% of $400,000)	100,000
Total preferred dividend	300,000

This leaves $900,000 of profits ($1,200,000 - $300,000) for paying a dividend to common stockholders and for re-investing in the business through retained profits.

The characteristics of participating preferred stock, providing a minimum dividend to the investor plus a share in surplus profits, make this type of share well suited to many business venture financings. The advantages of participating preferred stock to a venture capitalist are that

- if the company's profits are insufficient to pay the preferred dividend, the company is not in default on any borrowing obligations. The dividend is simply not paid and, if the stocks are cumulative as well as participating, the dividend is rolled up and will become payable when the company's profits are sufficient to pay them.
- the shareholder (venture capitalist) is entitled to a minimum annual dividend, provided that profits are sufficient to pay it. In addition, the venture capitalist can benefit from an enhanced dividend if the company's business is a success.

Deferred Consideration

In a buyout or buy-in, the seller of the business could agree to postpone (defer) some of the payment. This deferred consideration takes the form of a loan to the buyout company that is possibly interest-free, and redeemable on or before an agreed future date.

For example, a parent company might sell a business operation to a buyout team for \$5 million, and agree to defer \$1 million of the payment for three years. If the buyout team establishes a new company, the deferred payment would take the form of a loan to the new company, redeemable after three years with interest payable at an agreed rate.

Senior Debt

Senior debt is secured lending. The lender ranks ahead of other creditors of the company in the event of its liquidation and can, if required, seek payment for amounts owed (debt principal and arrears of interest) from the forced sale of the secured assets.

Secured debt finance is provided by banks, and is usually a major element in the financing package for a business venture. During the downturn in the early 1990s, banks experienced high bad-debt levels on loans to businesses, particularly in the US and the UK. Although bank lending has since recovered, banks remain very conscious of their exposure to credit risks. As a result banks often will not provide loans for a venture where the gearing ratio, measured as the ratio of secured and unsecured loans to share capital, exceeds 50%.

Banks generally will restrict their lending to a sum that is secured by assets, or in some cases to a sum that is secured on cash flows. This can cause problems for companies with low asset backing or with no independent profit history.

Companies also must be expected to generate sufficient cash flows to meet their debt payment obligations, for both secured and unsecured debt. Senior debt provided to business ventures, including MBOs, will carry a higher rate of interest than conventional term loans advanced to established businesses.

Caps and Collars

When loans are provided to a venture at a floating rate of interest, the borrower is exposed to the risk that interest rates will rise. If the rise in interest rates is steep, the company could struggle to meet its debt payment obligations.

In some venture agreements, the company limits its exposure to this interest rate risk by purchasing a cap or a collar.

- A cap is an agreement, usually with the lending bank, to set a maximum limit on the effective interest rate that will be payable on a floating rate loan. If interest rates rise above the level of the cap, the bank compensates the borrower under the cap agreement, so that the net interest charge is restricted to the cap level.
- A collar is an agreement to set both a maximum limit – a cap – and a minimum limit – a floor – on the effective interest rate payable on a floating-rate loan.

A collar gives some protection to the bank against falling interest rates, and guarantees a minimum return on the lending. Because the bank obtains this protection, it is cheaper for the borrower to arrange a collar than a cap.

Subordinated Debt

Subordinated debt is debt that ranks after senior debt in entitlement to repayment in the event of the company's liquidation. Subordinated loans could be secured either by a second charge on the company's assets, or unsecured. In a venture capital financing, banks providing senior loans could be willing to allow venture capitalists to provide some subordinated loans, although they could be concerned about excessive leverage.

The advantages of subordinated debt are that

- like preferred stock, they provide the venture capitalist with a regular annual income (interest)
- interest on debt is allowable for tax purposes, unlike dividends on preferred stock.

Mezzanine Finance

Mezzanine finance is debt finance that ranks below senior debt but ahead of equity in entitlement to payment in the event of the company's liquidation. It is therefore subordinated loan stock or junior loan stock.

The term mezzanine finance was developed in the UK in the mid-1980s to describe arrangements that provided a layer between senior debt and equity in the financing package. In general terms, it lies somewhere between equity and senior debt on the risk/reward scale. It can include high-yielding subordinated debt with no equity rights, and zero-coupon bonds with substantial equity conversion rights.

As compensation for the higher credit risk, the interest rate on mezzanine finance is usually a few percentage points higher than on senior debt, typically 1% to 3% higher, but sometimes more. In addition, mezzanine finance often carries an equity kicker giving the lender the right to obtain an equity stake in the company.

Kickers

A kicker is an additional incentive.

- An equity kicker gives the loan provider an entitlement to subscribe for common stock in the company at a future date. Normally it will take the form of either share options or share warrants.
- A non-equity kicker gives the loan provider an extra payment, for example a premium on redemption of the loan at maturity, or a fee paid at redemption (a back-end loan fee).

The combination of the interest yield on the mezzanine debt and the expected returns from the equity kicker should offer a promised total return somewhere between the interest rate on the senior debt and the yield expected by institutional investors in the company's equity.

Key Characteristics of Mezzanine Finance

The key characteristics of mezzanine finance may be summarized as follows

- mezzanine finance is subordinate to senior debt, but gives the lender a higher interest yield
- in some agreements, particularly in the UK, the subordination is determined by a deed of priority
- an equity kicker is usually given to the lender in the form of share options or share warrants
- the yield required depends on market conditions and investors' perception of the risk. The total yield is the interest on the loan plus the profits from the equity kicker
- the exact proportion of mezzanine finance varies in each case, because it is generally taken on to fill a financing gap between senior debt and equity
- lenders will require various covenants from the company. Financial

covenants are likely to include a minimum interest cover requirement. Lenders also will expect the company to have good cash flows from its trading operations

- mezzanine may be short-term, interim financing.

Junk Bonds

In the US, and increasingly in Europe, there is an active market for junk bonds. These are unsecured debt securities issued by companies and purchased by investors in the bond markets. Junk bonds have a credit rating below investment grade, i.e. below BBB. Because they are high-risk debt securities, they carry a high rate of interest.

In the mid-to-late 1980s, much activity in the junk bond market was driven by leveraged buyouts. Companies used as buyout (or buy-in) vehicles issued junk bonds to finance the buyout. Some investment banks, notably Drexel Burnham Lambert, encouraged institutional investors to support junk bond issues in return for the high interest yields they offered.

The junk bond market suffered a setback in 1989 when Drexel Burnham Lambert filed for bankruptcy. Moreover, the number of business failures of companies that had issued high-yield bonds highlighted the riskiness of this type of investment. A survey carried out by Standard & Poor's between 1981 and 1996 showed that the likelihood of a borrower defaulting increased dramatically when debt was below investment grade, 27% compared to 4% on bonds issued above BBB-.

In the US, high-yield bonds have continued to be a feature of buyout financing, although they represent a much smaller part of the overall package. In Europe they have started to reappear in the late 1990s, partly because they are cheaper than mezzanine debt. In the UK, tax changes favor bond issues, and in general there is no obligation to give away equity kickers or repay any principal before maturity.

Deciding the Financing Structure

The financial package for a business venture is assembled as negotiations continue between the venture capitalist, the entrepreneur and other potential lenders and investors. Agreement has to be reached on how much finance is needed and also on what form it should take.

Amount of Finance Required

When the business plan is drawn up, the entrepreneur or management team will have made a forecast of how much financing will be required. In the case of a start-up or expansion scheme, the funding will have to cover capital expenditures, set-up costs and initial running costs. These can be estimated in the financial projections for the business plan.

In the case of a buyout, the total amount of funding will be less certain, but the management team should have

- an agreement in principle from the seller for the buyout, and
- a rough idea of the price.

The buyout price must be affordable. It is essential that the company should be able to meet its debt payment obligations out of its own internally generated operational cash flows.

A venture capitalist could disagree with the management's business plan about how much finance will be required to support a venture. In a buyout, for example, the venture capitalist could disagree with the estimate for capital expenditure, and write in a different (higher) figure.

The venture capitalist's views on post-buyout cash flows will affect the purchase price that it is willing to fund.

Valuation Methods

Two different valuations could be required

- the current value of the business, in the case of a buyout
- the anticipated value of the company at a future date, assuming the targets in the business plan are met. The future date for the valuation could be the earliest time at which the venture capitalists expect to exit and realize a profit on their investment.

There are several methods that a venture capitalist could use to value a buyout business

- a price/earnings ratio
- discounting the value of anticipated returns
- the realizable value of the business assets or the net asset (balance sheet) value of the business.

The valuation of LBOs can be much more complex and is discussed in the next chapter.

Price/Earnings Ratio

A company could be expected to achieve a fairly substantial level of profits from the outset. This is often the case, for example, with buyouts and buy-ins. A value for the business can be obtained from a price/earnings ratio (P/E ratio).

A price/earnings ratio is the ratio of a company's current market value to its annual earnings (broadly, profits after tax and preferred dividends). P/E ratios are available for quoted companies with a known share price but not for private companies, e.g. new business ventures. However, the P/E ratios for similar-quoted companies can be used to estimate a suitable P/E ratio for a private company.

The total value of the business will be

Value = Annual Earnings x P/E Ratio

An unquoted company's shares, i.e. shares in a business venture, usually should be valued on a lower P/E ratio than for a quoted company, because

- stocks in an unquoted company are illiquid
- an unquoted company is often smaller than similar quoted companies, and its commercial risks could therefore be higher
- an unquoted company usually has a shorter track record of earning profits than an established quoted company.

An unquoted company could be valued on a higher P/E ratio than a similar quoted company when

- its expected annual growth rate in profits is much higher
- it operates in a market niche with strong growth potential
- there is competition between venture capitalists to provide finance for the company.

Example
A management team wants to buy out the assets of their business division from the parent company and approach a venture capitalist. In discussions about the business plan, it is agreed that sustainable earnings of the buyout company will be $300,000 per annum, with good prospects for growth.

Similar quoted companies in the same industry have price/earnings ratios between 10 and 14.

Analysis
The venture capitalist could suggest a price/earnings ratio valuation of the business, based on the P/E ratios of quoted companies. Given a range of P/E ratios of between 10 and 14 for quoted companies, a suitable P/E ratio for an unquoted company would be 70% of this, in the range seven to 9.8. Because the company has good growth prospects, a P/E ratio towards the upper end of this range might be selected. If a P/E ratio of nine were chosen, the valuation of the business would be

Annual earnings x P/E Ratio = $300,000 x 9 = $2,700,000

The venture capitalist would not want the total investment to exceed this amount, and would indicate its intention to the management team. This valuation, if agreed, would form a basis for negotiating

- a buyout price from the parent company, and
- a financing structure for the buyout company.

Discounting Future Earnings

A venture capitalist organization usually expects an average rate of return from its investment in a business venture. The expected return should compensate the investor for the risks. Consequently the required return on common stock will be higher than the return on preferred stock that have a lower investment risk. Similarly, the required return on preferred share investments is higher than the return on unsecured loans. Taken together, however, average expected returns on a venture capitalist's investment could be in the region of 20% or 25% per annum or higher. In an individual venture, however, the required returns could be lower, or much higher, depending on

- the nature of the investment
- the stage of investment
- the perceived risk
- the financing package, and
- the number of years funds will be tied up in the investment before an exit becomes feasible.

The expected returns on an equity investment will consist of dividends on the shares, and the sale value of the shares at the exit date. The sale value of common stock at the exit date, however, can be estimated only. A suitable estimating method would be to multiply the company's expected earnings by an appropriate P/E ratio.

Discounting mathematics can be used to convert future cash returns to a present value. A present value represents an amount of money that must be invested now, at a given investment rate of return (IRR), to earn a future cash return at a given date.

$$PV = S_n \times \frac{1}{(1 + r)_n}$$

where

- PV is the present value of the future cash return
- S_n is the cash return, in year n
- r is the investor's required investment rate of return (IRR) expressed as a proportion (20% = 0.20, 45% = 0.45, etc.)
- n is the year at the end of which the cash return will be earned.

Example
A venture capital organization is considering a business venture that would be financed partly by equity and partly by convertible preferred stock. The total investment, including the entrepreneur's stake, will be around $2 million.

Preferred stock will be convertible into common stock after five years, on the basis of one $1 preferred share for one $1 common share. Preferred dividend will be 10% per annum.

It is estimated that the company's profits after tax will be $650,000 per annum after five years.

The company will not expect to pay a dividend on common stock for two years, but should pay a dividend of 10% per annum from the third year onwards.

It has been agreed that after five years, the company will seek a stock market listing. At this time, the venture capital organization will convert the preferred stock into common stock, and sell all its shares in the flotation. A P/E ratio of 12 could be achieved in the flotation.

It has also been agreed that the management/entrepreneurs in the venture should hold the common share capital in the ratio 60:40 with the venture capitalist. Management will provide $600,000 in capital.

The venture capitalist's required returns on the total investment are 30% per annum.

Analysis

Suppose the negotiated capital structure is as follows:

	$	
Management holding of 600,000 common stock	600,000	(60%)
Venture capitalist's holding of 400,000 common stock	400,000	(40%)
10% preferred stock	1,000,000	
	2,000,000	

At the end of five years, the company's earnings will be $650,000 per annum. (The preference dividend can be ignored because the preferred stock will be converted into common stock.) The market capitalization of the company on flotation therefore should be

	Earnings x P/E ratio
=	$650,000 x 12
=	$7,800,000
=	$3.90 per share ($7.8 million ÷ two million shares)

The venture capitalist, on converting the preferred stock, will hold 70% of the equity (1.4 million shares out of two million). The value of the shares at exit will be $5.46 million (1.4 million shares at $3.90 per share).

The value of the expected returns to the venture capitalist is the present value of the preferred dividends and common stock dividends in each year, from years 1 to 5, plus the present value of the eventual sale price of the shares. The dividends and sale value should be discounted at the venture capitalist's IRR of 30% per annum.

Year	Preferred dividend	Common stock dividend	Sale of shares	Total return	Discount factor at 30%	Present value
	$m	$m	$m	$m		$m
1	0.10	-	-	0.10	$1/(1.30)^1$	0.08
2	0.10	-	-	0.10	$1/(1.30)^2$	0.06
3	0.10	0.06	-	0.16	$1/(1.30)^3$	0.07
4	0.10	0.06	-	0.16	$1/(1.30)^4$	0.06
5	0.10	0.06	5.46	5.62	$1/(1.30)^5$	1.51
			Present value of future returns			1.78

The venture capitalist is considering an investment of $1.4 million in the company. The present value of the future returns is higher, $1.78 million, indicating that the return on investment will exceed the target IRR of 30% per annum.

Asset Values

A venture capital organization occasionally could consider the asset value of a company in which it has been asked to invest. However, asset values are an unreliable guide to business valuations. The returns earned by a business provide the investment value, not the assets themselves. In some cases, the assets of a loss-making business could have a substantial sale value (net realizable value). There could, for example, be some land and buildings involved. If such a business is available to a buyout or buy-in team, its valuation could not be less than the net realizable value of its assets. This is the minimum price that the seller could obtain by selling off the assets themselves.

Contributors to the Financing Package

The financing package for a business venture is normally structured by the lead venture capitalist. The entrepreneur or management team can negotiate points of detail or even refuse the venture capitalist's offer. It has to be recognized, however, that the venture capitalist will want a minimum expected return for the investment risk, and will propose a financing structure that satisfies this objective.

There is no single unique solution to deciding a financing structure. Each venture capital organization will have its own views on what appears to be appropriate.

In some ventures, the financing could be simply an all-equity investment by the venture capitalist. A small company could have drawn up plans for expansion and to raise the finance necessary by issuing common stock to a venture capitalist.

Venture Capitalist's Stake

A distinction should be made between the role of a venture capitalist as provider of finance from its own fund, and its role as lead manager in financing a venture, assembling a syndicate of venture capitalist backers and raising loans from banks.

A venture capitalist could be willing to invest funds in a business in the form of common stock, preferred, and/or subordinated loans. However, it will also arrange finance from other sources, primarily banks and other venture capital investors.

Normally banks will be asked to provide funds in the form of senior debt, should debt finance be required. Lending banks must be convinced that the company will be able to meet its debt repayment obligations from its operational cash flows, as well as obtaining adequate security. Institutional investors could also be invited to participate by investing in high-yield bonds of the company.

Entrepreneur's Stake

To convince financial backers of their commitment to the venture, the entrepreneurs or management team will be expected to invest some of its own money in the venture, in return for a significant portion of the equity in the business. It could be necessary to obtain a personal loan to raise the capital.

There are several reasons why the total amount invested by the entrepreneurs/management team is small, relative to the size of their common stockholding.

- They are usually unable to provide more finance, and often have to seek personal loans to raise their share of the funding.
- They provide the original business idea and/or will contribute significantly to its success.
- They are risking their career and financial security in the venture, and should be rewarded accordingly.

Earn-out

In a venture-financing negotiation, the venture capitalist could be prepared to offer incentives to management to motivate them towards making the venture successful. Incentives can take the form of an earn-out.

An earn-out is an arrangement whereby managers get a larger share of the company's equity if the business performs well and achieves certain specified targets in the business plan. The earn-out allows the exact division of the common stock capital between the entrepreneurs and the venture capitalists to be decided after the success (or failure) of the venture is known.

Example
A company is the subject of a management buyout. It is making annual after-tax profits of $2 million that are forecast to rise to $5 million after three years. The venture capital organization financing the buyout has estimated that to achieve its target return on investment, it would have to own 40% of the company's common stock capital if annual profits were $5 million at the end of three years. However, if annual profits are $6 million, it will have to own about 30% of the ordinary share capital to earn its target return.

Analysis
A earn-out arrangement could be agreed whereby for every $100,000 of profits over $5 million per annum after three years, up to a ceiling of $6 million, management should be entitled to an extra half percent of the equity. If profits reach $6 million, management will raise their stake in the ordinary share capital from 60% to 65%.

Earn-outs can be both upward and downward. If profits are below a target amount, management could be required to give more of the equity to the venture capitalist.

Earn-outs operate by means of convertible redeemable preferred stock held by the venture capitalist. Management's stake in the equity could be increased, under the earn-out agreement, by redeeming the shares and the venture capitalist choosing not to convert them into common stock. Earn-outs also might be in the form of options to buy new shares at a price below their current value. The exercise date for the options is linked to the payment of a cash bonus to management, who could then use the cash to pay for the new shares.

An earn-out is another form of incentive, and is a payment linked to the future performance of the company. For example, the amount of the payment could be a multiple of profits in excess of a certain target level, shared between the management team in agreed proportions.

Banks and Business Ventures

Although merchant banks/investment banks become involved in arranging a buyout (as lead manager), the principal role of banks in business ventures is to provide secured loans. Without debt finance, some ventures would not be financially worthwhile for the venture capitalist. The starting point for a financing structure could therefore be to decide the optimal amount of debt finance. This can be established, for example, by deciding an optimal (or minimum) interest cover ratio.

Example
A business is the subject of an MBO. Its profits before interest and tax (PBIT) are expected to be $2.4 million in the first year. The lead venture capitalist considers that the minimum interest cover ratio should be 2.0 times. (This is the ratio of PBIT to interest costs.) The interest rate on loans would be 12% per annum.

Analysis
The interest cover ratio should not be less than 2.0 times. This means that if PBIT is $2.4 million per annum, interest charges should not exceed $1.2 million ($2.4m ÷ 2.0). If interest will be payable at 12%, the maximum amount of debt capital the company should obtain is $10 million ($10 million x 12% = $1.2 million).

In recent years, banks have managed their lending to business ventures in much the same way as their other business lending, i.e. they

- make their own assessment of the business plan
- learn what they can about the business and the company's management
- get to know the venture capitalist who is backing the company
- discuss with management their expectations of obtaining additional bank loans or facilities, as the company expands
- satisfy themselves that the financial controls of the business and management reporting systems are satisfactory
- obtain regular reports from the business about its financial position
- establish a relationship with the management of the business, through a bank liaison officer.

Credit analysis practices vary to some degree between banks, as well as over time. However, certain key financial ratios will be identified. The bank will expect the ratios to meet certain targets. Illustrative ratios and targets are suggested in the table below.

Key Credit Assessment Ratios

	Year 1	Year 2	Year 3	Year 4	Year 5
Total interest cover (Note 1)	1.70:1	1.80:1	2.00:1	2.25:1	2.50:1
Senior debt interest cover (Note 2)	2.0:1	2.20:1	2.50:1	3.00:1	3.25:1
Ratio of operating cash inflow: cash outflow	1.02:1	1.03:1	1.04:1	1.05:1	1.08:1
Gearing (debt:equity rates)	1:1	1:1	0.95:1	0.90:1	0.80:1
Loan repayment	5%	5%	10%	10%	20%

Notes:

(1) Interest cover is the ratio of profit before interest and tax to interest charges in the year, on all borrowing.

(2) Senior debt interest cover is the ratio of PBIT to interest charges in the year on senior debt.

Often companies will try to reduce their borrowings as soon as possible. Initially, the priority for repayment should be senior debt, provided that the arrangement cost for an early redemption of the loan is not high. If cash flow forecasts permit, it may be appropriate to arrange a stepped repayment loan, where repayments are made in stages, rather than a bullet loan where all the repayment is made at the end of the term.

Structuring the Financing Package

Each financing is unique, and can involve a different structure of common stock, preferred stock, senior loans, subordinated loans and bank facilities such as an overdraft. Often the various investors will set up a shell company. The shell company then purchases the buyout business, either by acquiring the shares of the target company or selected assets and liabilities.

The sale of business assets is achieved by the seller transferring the assets to the newly established company, financed by an inter-company loan. The buyout team then purchases the company, and pays the seller by means of repaying the company loan. Transferring assets to a new company for the purpose of a buyout is known as a hive down.

Because financing packages may differ quite widely, it will be useful to study a few examples.

Example 1

A management team of six executives approached a venture capitalist for support in buying their food-processing business from the parent company. The venture capitalist was willing to back the venture.

The purchase price would be $2 million, but the parent company was willing to defer $600,000 of the purchase consideration, by granting a four-year unsecured loan at 4% interest to the buyout company.

The management team determined that it would be able to provide $100,000.

Analysis
The management team wants the venture capitalist to assemble a financial package for the $2 million buyout, and can offer $100,000 of their own money and $600,000 from the seller as a four-year loan costing $24,000 (4%) per annum in interest. This leaves $1.3 million of finance to be raised.

The venture capitalist will study the cash flow and profit projections of the business to decide how much finance could be raised in the form of secured bank loans. The company's ability to borrow depends on

- the security it can offer for loans
- the strength of its operational cash flows, and
- the maximum level of gearing that lending banks will approve.

Suppose that the venture capitalist is able to arrange $400,000 of secured loans at 10% interest from a small group of banks that do not wish to see gearing rise above 50%.

The remaining $900,000 would have to be provided as venture capital, in the form of common stock, preferred stock and possibly unsecured loans. A small syndicate of venture capitalists could be brought together, each willing to invest up to a certain amount in the business. The mix of common stock, preferred stock and unsecured loans will depend on

- the returns that the business is expected to make, after allowing for interest payments on bank loans and the loan from the parent company (the seller's deferred consideration)
- the returns that the venture capitalists expect to receive on their investments in the form of common stock, preferred stock and unsecured loans
- the entitlements attached to the preferred stock or unsecured loans that could be convertible into common stock, and the preferred stock could be participating shares, giving the right to a share in excess profits of the company
- the appropriate equity stake for the management team.

The final package could, for example, have the following structure

	$
Common stock for management team	100,000
Common stock for venture capitalists	150,000
Preferred stock for venture capitalists	750,000
Secured bank loan	400,000
Unsecured loan from parent company	600,000
	2,000,000

This would give management 100,000 of the 250,000 common stock issued, i.e. 40% of the equity. Gearing (the debt:total capital ratio) would be 50% ($1 million ÷ $2 million x 100%).

Example 2
An entrepreneur wishes to continue a business venture in which he has already invested $30,000. A business plan is agreed with a venture capitalist in which the following funding requirements have been agreed.

	$
Set-up costs already incurred	30,000
Further costs of set-up	120,000
Plant and machinery	550,000
Equipment	200,000
Lease improvements	200,000
Working capital	
Stocks	70,000
Debtors	80,000
Finance to cover initial operating deficit	150,000
Total funding required	1,400,000

The venture capitalist suggests a mix of senior debt, finance leases, subordinated debt, preferred stock and common stock.

- The ratio of debt to share capital should not exceed 1:1.
- The entrepreneur should have a 60% stake in the common share capital, and will invest $120,000, including the $30,000 already spent.

- Plant and equipment with a valuation of $400,000 could be leased.
- Banks will provide secured loans on a borrowing base formula. The amounts advanced will be

	% of value
On $350,000 of machinery and equipment	50
On stocks	30
On debtors	60

Analysis

Secured bank loans would be available as follows:

	$
Secured on machinery and equipment (50% of $350,000)	175,000
Secured on stocks (30% of $70,000)	21,000
Secured on debtors (60% of $80,000)	48,000
	244,000

Total leverage in the $1.4 million funding should not exceed 50%; therefore the maximum debt is $700,000.

	$
Debt provided	
As lease finance	400,000
As secured loans	244,000
As subordinated loans (balance)	56,000
	700,000

The entrepreneur will invest $120,000, including the $30,000 already spent. If this will represent 60% of the common stock, the venture capitalist should acquire $80,000 (40%) of the common stock. Preference share capital should be $500,000, in order to make up the total funding.

A suggested financing package could be

	$000	$000
Common stock		
Entrepreneur	120	
Venture capitalist	80	
		200
Preferred stock (venture capitalists)		500
Total share capital		700
Finance leases	400	
Senior debt	244	
Subordinated debt	56	
Total debt capital		700
Total funding		1,400

Stage Financing

Stage financing involves an agreement by the venture capitalist to provide finance at two or more stages in the business venture when specific planning targets are met. For example, in a start-up venture, an initial round of finance could be provided to take a product up to the end of its development stage, and a second round of finance would then be provided for the product's market launch. A third round of financing might also be agreed, for example to fund an expansion of manufacturing capacity when annual sales exceed a certain volume.

Stage financing can have benefits for both the venture capitalist and the entrepreneur.

- For the venture capitalist, it minimizes the size of the investment at each stage of business development, and therefore limits the investment risk.
- For the entrepreneur, the limited initial investment by the venture capitalist should enable the entrepreneur to acquire a larger proportion of the company's equity.

Other Sources of Finance

There are a number of ways in which a buyout company can bring down its initial working capital requirement, and reduce its financing requirements. These might include:

- government grants or loans
- leasing or hire purchase of assets
- sale and leaseback of properties
- debt factoring and invoice discounting.

In addition, vendors may help to finance a buyout, either by accepting deferred consideration in the form of convertible loan stock or by retaining a minority interest in the business.

Exit Routes

Each venture capital organization has its own ideas about when it would like to realize its investment from a venture. Some could be willing to invest for the long term, but most expect to have an exit available after about four to six years. In the past, some financiers have expected an exit after two to three years, but in general these expectations have been regarded as over-optimistic.

Planning to exit and realize the investment is an integral part of negotiating the financial package for a venture. The entrepreneurs/management team must understand what the venture capitalist expects, and agree what the exit route should be. Most exit routes in the past have been through a trade sale.

The venture capitalist will estimate what the value of the investment could be at the exit date. The capital gain should provide a substantial return on the initial equity investment; otherwise the venture capitalist would not agree to support the venture by providing capital.

Stock Market Flotations

The availability of a stock market flotation as an exit route depends largely on stock market conditions. A significant rise in flotations on the London stock market in 1996/97 was attributed in part to venture capitalists seeking to take advantage of strong investor demand for equities that existed at the time.

When the flotation exit route for venture capitalists is not readily available, many hold on to their investments for a longer period. Alternatively, other exit routes could be sought, such as a trade sale or a secondary purchase.

Refinancing

Finding investors to purchase a venture capitalist's investment in a private company can be difficult. If a stock market flotation is not possible, and a trade buyer cannot be found, the option of refinancing has to be considered.

One example is Presswork Metals, that supplies components for safety belts, airbags and air condition units to the automotive industry. Presswork was the subject of a $10 million MBO in 1989. In 1997 the original syndicate of four institutional investors was seeking to exit the company. The management did not want to sacrifice the company's independence by selling to a trade buyer or floating on the stock exchange, and so a re-engineered $16 million MBO was arranged, whereby the investments of the original institutions were repaid and replaced.

8

LBO Finance

During the 1980s and 1990s, a number of specialist buyout institutions emerged that raised funds dedicated to financing leveraged buyouts.

- Target companies were acquired, partly with finance from buyout funds and partly by issuing junk bonds.
- The acquired company, often a quoted company, reverted to private company status.
- Such acquisitions often followed successful hostile bids. The price that could be offered was high enough to win shareholder acceptances, despite resistance to the buyout from the target company's management.

The effect of an LBO on the purchased company is that its capital structure becomes much more highly leveraged and equity is replaced by debt. As a result, the valuation of the company will change, even though its underlying business remains the same as before the buyout.

LBO specialists would argue that the total value of the company should be enhanced by higher leverage, so that it would be worth more after the LBO.

LBO Valuation

A problem for the buyout institution in a leveraged buyout is estimating the company's value after the buyout. The buyout price should not exceed this value. However, its value cannot be easily determined, because the purchased company will not have a stockmarket listing after the LBO.

A valuation can be made using discounted cash flow techniques. The expected future returns on investment can be discounted to a present value, at the investor's required investment rate of return (IRR) per annum.

Cost of Debt Capital

The cost of debt capital in an LBO is the interest yield required by the providers of debt finance. With floating rate loans, the cost of debt could be about two to three percentage points above the London Interbank Offered Rate (LIBOR). For example, if six-month LIBOR is 8% per annum and lending is at 2% above six-month LIBOR, the initial cost of borrowing would be 10% per annum.

Interest on loans can be an allowable expense for tax purposes, and this tax shield has the effect of reducing the amount of tax payable on profits. The value of the tax shield is the amount of interest payable multiplied by the rate of corporation tax. For example, if interest on loans of $100 million is $10 million, i.e. 10%, and the rate of tax is 30%, the value of the tax shield is $3 million (30%).

The cost of debt capital allowing for the tax shield, i.e. the net of tax cost of debt, is

$$R_d = i\,(1 - t)$$

Where

- R_d is the net of tax cost of debt
- i is the interest rate (gross)
- t is the rate of corporation tax, as a proportion, e.g. 30% = 0.30.

When the gross interest cost is 10%, for example, and the rate of corporation tax is 30%, the after-tax cost of debt is 10% (1 - 0.30) = 7%.

Cost of Equity

The cost of equity is the average annual return on investment that equity stockholders expect to receive. It is higher in high-leveraged companies than in low-leveraged companies, to compensate shareholders for the greater financial risk.

One method of estimating the cost of equity is the Capital Asset Pricing Model (CAPM). The principles underlying the CAPM are beyond the scope of this book. The model is explained in more detail in *Capital Structuring*, another title in this series. Briefly, a special factor, called a beta factor, can be calculated for the shares of each individual quoted company. Beta factors are calculated from a mathematical analysis of dividend returns and share price movements.

The CAPM is a formula that relates a company's cost of equity to its beta factor, as follows:

$$R_e = R_f + ß(R_m - R_f)$$

Where

- R_e is the company's cost of equity
- R_f is a risk-free rate of return based on the current yield on domestic government bonds
- ß is the beta factor
- R_m is the current average returns on stock market investments.

For example, if the current risk-free rate of return is 7% and average market returns are 11%, the expected return on the equity capital of a company with a beta factor of 0.9 will be:

$$R_e \quad = 7\% + 0.9\ (11\% - 7\%) \quad = 10.6\%$$

Leveraged and Unleveraged Betas

The CAPM can be used to estimate the change in the cost of a company's equity if its level of leverage changes. A mathematical relationship can be established between

- the cost of equity in a company with no gearing, an unleveraged company, and
- the cost of equity in an identical company, except that it is partly financed by debt, a leveraged company.

The beta factor of the leveraged company is higher than the beta factor of the unleveraged company because the financial risk is higher and shareholders will expect a higher return on investment. The relationship between the beta factors in a leveraged company and a similar unleveraged company is shown in the following formula.

$$ß_g = ß_u [1 + (1 - t) D/E]$$

Where

- $ß_g$ is the beta factor of a leveraged company
- $ß_u$ is the beta factor of an identical unleveraged company
- t is the rate of corporation tax
- D/E is the ratio of debt to equity finance in the leveraged company's capital structure.

To estimate the change in a company's beta factor as a consequence of an LBO, we can

- convert the company's current beta factor ($ß_g$) to an unleveraged beta factor ($ß_u$) using the formula. If the company is a quoted company, its beta factor at the buyout date should be known.
- convert the unleveraged beta ($ß_u$) to a new leveraged beta ($ß_g$), to reflect the higher gearing level of the company.

The new beta factor can then be used to estimate the cost of equity in the LBO company.

Example
Alpha Inc, a quoted US company, is the subject of a $100 million LBO. Alpha Inc was entirely financed by equity before the buyout, and its beta factor was 0.8. After the buyout, the company is financed by 80% debt and 20% equity.

Corporation tax is 30%. Average stock-market returns are 8% and the risk-free rate of return is 5%. The cost of the debt capital for the LBO company is 7% (gross).

Analysis

Before the LBO, Alpha's cost of equity, estimated from the CAPM formula, was

$$R_e = 5\% + 0.8\ (8\% - 5\%) \qquad = 7.4\%$$

After the LBO, the beta factor of the company will increase. The new beta factor will be:

$$ß_g = 0.8\ [1 + (1 - 0.3)\ 80/20] = 0.8\ (1 + 2.8) = 3.04$$

The cost of equity capital of Alpha after the LBO, using the CAPM formula again, is therefore

$$R_e = 5\% + 3.04\ (8\% - 5\%) = 14.12\%$$

This suggests that whereas the cost of equity in Alpha before the LBO was 7.4%, it has risen after the LBO to about 14.1%. Equity shareholders now expect a much higher rate of return on their investment.

Weighted Average Cost of Capital

The valuation of a business after an LBO can be made by estimating the future returns from the company after the buyout, and discounting them at the investor's required investment rate of return (IRR).

If the same investor finances the entire LBO, a valuation can be obtained by discounting the company's net operating cash flows over the investment period at the weighted average IRR of the investment funds. This is the LBO company's weighted average cost of funds.

A weighted average cost of funds is

$$\left[R_d x \frac{D}{(D + E)}\right] + \left[R_e x \frac{E}{(D + E)}\right]$$

Where

- R_d is the after-tax cost of debt capital
- R_e is the cost of equity capital
- D is the amount of debt finance in the capital structure
- E is the amount of equity finance in the capital structure.

Example

In the previous example of Alpha Inc, the weighted average cost of capital for the company, i.e. the average IRR of investment funds in the LBO company, is as follows:

Cost of debt (gross)	7%
Corporation tax	30%
After-tax cost of debt, Rd	7% (1 - 0.3) i.e. 4.9%
Cost of equity after increase in gearing	14.12%

Weighted average cost of capital:

$$\left[4.9\% \times \frac{80}{100}\right] + \left[14.12\% \times \frac{20}{100}\right]$$

$$= 3.92\% + 2.824\%$$

$$= 6.744\%, \text{ or approx. } 6.75\%$$

The average cost of funds is lower for the company after the LBO when it is highly leveraged, than before when it was low-leveraged. This is because of the effect of the tax shield on debt interest. The average cost of Alpha's funds has fallen from 7.4% before the LBO to 6.75% after the LBO.

Making an LBO Valuation (Weighted Average Cost of Funds Method)

The weighted average cost of funds can be used to make a valuation of a company after an LBO. The estimated future annual net operating cash flows of the company should be discounted to a present value using the weighted average cost of funds as the required yield. Net operating cash flows can be estimated as the annual profits before interest and tax (PBIT) plus depreciation, that is a non-cash charge against profits.

PBIT + Depreciation = Net operating cash flows

If the net operating cash flows are a constant amount every year, the valuation mathematics are simplified, and the present value of the investment is

$$\frac{CF}{r}$$

Where

- CF is the annual net operating cash flows, and
- r is the weighted average cost of funds.

Example

Returning again to the example of Alpha Inc, suppose the net operating cash flows of the company are expected to be $10 million per year for the first two years, and $12 million per year from the third year onwards, as the benefits of a rationalization program take effect.

The buyout investment institution wishes to value the company on the basis of its operating cash flows for four years, plus the estimated value of the company at the end of the fourth year, when a reflotation on the stock market is planned. An estimated market valuation at the end of the fourth year is $120 million.

The company's weighted average cost of funds is 6.75%.

Analysis

Using the weighted average cost of funds as the IRR, the valuation of Alpha immediately after the LBO would be as follows

Year	Item	Amount	Discount factor at 6.75% per annum	Present value
		$m		$m
1	Net operating cash flows	10	$\frac{1}{(1.0675)}$	9.37
2	Net operating cash flows	10	$\frac{1}{(1.0675)2}$	8.78
3	Net operating cash flows	12	$\frac{1}{(1.0675)3}$	9.86

4	Net operating cash flows	12	$\frac{1}{(1.0675)4}$	9.24
5	Flotation value	120	1 (1.0675)4	92.41
				129.66

On these estimates, the total valuation of Alpha would be about $130 million after the LBO.

Making an LBO Valuation: Alternative Method

The valuation of an LBO company based on the weighted average cost of capital depends for its validity on the assumption that the company's leveraging level will remain unchanged over the investment period. Therefore its weighted average cost of capital will be unchanged. This is unlikely to be the case for an LBO company that often will reduce its leveraging as soon as possible, repaying debt from its operational cash surpluses to reduce the financial risk.

An alternative method of valuation for an LBO company therefore could be more appropriate. This alternative method is based on the theory that the total value of a leveraged company is higher than the total value of an identical unleveraged (all-equity) company. The value of a leveraged company is the sum of

- the value of the company if it were all-equity (unleveraged), plus
- the present value of the tax shield, i.e. the value of the lower tax payments due to interest charges being an allowable cost against tax.

Example
The example of Alpha Inc will be used again.

Alpha Inc is expected to have the following net operating cash flows

Year	Net operating cash flows
	$m
1	10
2	10
3	12
4	12

At the end of the fourth year, Alpha Inc will be floated on the stock market at an estimated value of $120 million.

The cost of equity for Alpha as an unleveraged company is 7.4%. Alpha's cost of equity after the LBO will be 14.12%. The pre-tax cost of debt in the LBO company is 7%, and total borrowings of Alpha are $80 million. The rate of corporation tax is 30%.

Analysis

The value of Alpha as an all-equity company can be established by discounting the expected cash flows from the investment. The discount rate should be the cost of equity in Alpha if it were an unleveraged company. This is 7.4%.

Year	Item	Amount	Discount factor at 7.4% per annum	Present value
		$m		$m
1	Net operating cash flows	10	$\frac{1}{(1.074)^1}$	9.31
2	Net operating cash flows	10	$\frac{1}{(1.074)^2}$	8.67
3	Net operating cash flows	12	$\frac{1}{(1.074)^3}$	9.69
4	Net operating cash flows	12	$\frac{1}{(1.074)^4}$	9.02
4	Flotation value	120	$\frac{1}{(1.074)^4}$	90.19
			All-equity valuation	126.88

The debt of Alpha is $80 million, and with interest at 7% per annum, interest charges can be estimated as $5.6 million each year (7% of $80m). This cost is allowable against tax; therefore there is a cash benefit to Alpha each year from the lower amount of tax payable, as follows

Interest	$5.6 million
Tax rate	30%
Reduction in tax payable	$1.68 million (30% of $5.6m)

Alpha will benefit from this lower tax payment each year up to flotation. The present value of this cash benefit should be calculated by discounting the tax saving at the pre-tax cost of debt, 7%.

Year	**Tax saved** $m	**Discount factor at 7%**	**Present value** $m
1	1.68	$\frac{1}{(1.07)}$	1.57
2	1.68	$\frac{1}{(1.07)^2}$	1.47
3	1.68	$\frac{1}{(1.07)^3}$	1.37
4	1.68	$\frac{1}{(1.07)^4}$	1.28
			5.69

The total valuation of Alpha to the investment buyers of the company, after the LBO, is therefore estimated as follows

	$m
Value of Alpha as all-equity company	126.88
Value of tax shield	5.69
Total value of Alpha after the LBO	132.57

This method gives a slightly higher valuation than the valuation based on the weighted average cost of capital.

Structuring an LBO

In the mid-1980s, when interest rates were fairly low in the US, buyout companies generally could afford higher levels of debt. Higher debt, applying the valuation principles described in this chapter, implies a higher value for the company. It was therefore in the interests of investors – subject to an acceptable level of financial risk for debt providers – to increase gearing in an LBO company to the highest level possible.

An LBO financing therefore could involve a debt:equity ratio as high as 9:1 during those years, when the financing mix could have been

Senior debt	circa 60-70%
Mezzanine finance	circa 20-30%
Equity	circa 10%

However, as interest rates rose in the later 1980s such high levels of leveraging could not be sustained, and a higher proportion of equity funding was required for subsequent LBOs.

Ratchets in LBOs

Ratchet mechanisms have been common in LBO financings. The venture capitalist could subscribe for convertible preferred stock or convertible loan stock, with the exercise date for conversion timed to coincide with the planned exit date (normally flotation). Usually the ratchet is based on value at exit, but may also relate to the time of exit.

Example

In an LBO financing, it is agreed that management should hold 25% of the ordinary share capital and a venture capitalist syndicate the remaining 75%, together with some convertible redeemable preference shares.

Analysis

A ratchet mechanism should be introduced as follows. It could be agreed that if the value of the company on flotation gives the venture capitalist a return on investment of 50% per annum or more, the preference shares would be redeemed on flotation. However, if the return on investment is between 40% and 50% per annum, one half of the preferred stock will be redeemed and one half converted, reducing management's share of common stock to 15%. As the venture capitalist's share of common stock increases, its share of the returns from the growth of the company increases, enhancing the IRR on its investment. If the return on investment is less than 40%, all the preferred stock will be converted, reducing management's stake in the common stock to 5%.

9

Venture Capital Portfolios and Portfolio Valuations

Venture capitalists need to make a profit on their investments. In the case of a venture capital fund, investors in the fund expect to make a profit when the fund's investments in ventures are eventually realized and the sale proceeds distributed. In the case of a venture capital company there is a similar requirement to make sure that the investment portfolio will generate profits to cover its borrowing costs and pay dividends to shareholders. Some concern has been expressed about the disappointing performance of venture capital funds. However, it has been difficult for external investors to assess fund performance properly. This is because venture funds have had considerable leeway in the way they report their results, although guidelines on measuring fund performance have been issued by various associations.

IRR Calculations

Although portfolio valuations are necessary to monitor the value of current investments, the key measure of performance for investors is the rate of return actually achieved on each individual investment between the date of investment and the date of realization. This can be calculated as the investment rate of return/internal rate of return (IRR). The IRR on investment is illustrated in chapters 2 and 7.

Realized and Unrealized Profits

The profits of a venture capital organization arise largely from interest and dividends received on loans to ventures and share capital investments. However, a part of its profits come from the realization of investments, i.e. the eventual sale of shares on exit. The realized profit on an investment is simply the eventual sale value less the initial cost.

Capital gains are realized only at exit, typically several years after the initial investment. The value of the investment should rise year by year from the start of the venture until the exit date. Profits occur as the investment rises in value, but are unrealized until the eventual sale.

Example

A venture capitalist invested $2 million in a company. Over the next four years, the investment's value was assessed as follows:

End of year	Estimated value
	$m
1	2.2
2	2.5
3	3.5
4	5.0

At the start of the fifth year, the investment was sold in a trade sale for $5 million.

Analysis

The profit on the investment could be measured each year as

Year	Unrealized profit	Realized profit
	$m	$m
1 ($2.2m - $2m)	0.2	-
2 ($2.5m - $2.2m)	0.3	-
3 ($3.5m - $2.5m)	1.0	-
4 ($5m - $3.5)	1.5	-
5 ($5m - $2m)		3.0

The realized profit in Year 5 consists of the estimated, accumulated unrealized profits up to the time of the sale.

Measuring realized profits is necessary for two reasons:

- to determine the venture capitalist's reported profits in the year of realization, and
- to measure the actual returns on the investment to ensure that actual returns on average are continuing to meet the venture capitalist's target criteria for investment returns.

Measuring unrealized profits – an investment's current value – is thought necessary

- for financial reporting, to include the venture capitalist's investment portfolio in the balance sheet at its estimated current value, and
- to reassure fund investors/shareholders about the value of the venture capitalist's investments.

Valuation Principles

It is recommended that investments in ordinary shares in a venture capital portfolio should be grouped into three broad categories, and that a different set of valuation principles applied to each. The three categories are

- unquoted venture investments
- unquoted development investments
- quoted investments.

Unquoted Venture Investments

An unquoted venture investment is an investment in an immature private company that is at the seedcorn, start-up or early stage of development. Because of the immaturity of these investments, and uncertainty about their eventual success, it is recommended that in most cases they should be valued at cost, rather than at an estimated market valuation.

In some cases an unquoted venture investment could be revalued upwards. This is acceptable in any of three circumstances

- the company has had a further stage financing involving a large third-party investment. This could be an investment by another venture capitalist that has valued the company at a significantly higher amount
- the company is normally valued on the basis of its net assets, and the net asset value exceeds the investment cost
- the company is already earning significant profits.

A revaluation below investment cost should be made when

- the company's results are significantly below what were the original projections
- the company is in financial difficulties and requires additional funding to survive.

Downward valuations of an investment should be in no more than three discreet stages, for example, by 25%, 50% and 100%, or to net realizable value, or to a valuation provided by an independent third party. This simplification of devaluation is recommended because valuation involves a large degree of judgment, and more varied and complex valuation methods necessarily would not be more reliable.

Unquoted Development Investments

Unquoted development investments are investments in mature private companies that have achieved a maintainable level of profits, and where an exit – by flotation or trade sale – could be reasonably foreseen although not necessarily anticipated.

This type of investment can enter a venture capitalist's portfolio in either of two ways

- an unquoted venture investment becomes a development investment as the company grows successfully, or
- the venture capitalist invests in a development stage venture or private company buyout.

It could be appropriate to revalue these investments periodically to an estimated current market value, although not in the initial post-investment period, when the investment should remain valued at cost. A market valuation normally should be obtained by applying a price/earnings ratio to maintainable earnings, discounted to take account of the illiquid nature of the investment, the uncertainty about when the investment will become liquid, and the approximate nature of the valuation method.

The revaluation of unquoted development investments could be down as well as up, depending on the periodic assessment of maintainable earnings and the currently appropriate P/E ratio.

Quoted Investments

Quoted investments are investments still held by the venture capitalist in a company after it has obtained a stock market quotation. Quoted investments normally should be valued at their mid-market price at the valuation date.

In the case of illiquid quoted investments, a discount could be applied to the mid-market price valuation.

Loan Stock and Preferred Stock

Loan stock and preferred stock normally should be valued as fixed-interest securities. However,

- the valuation of a fixed-interest security can vary up or down, with changes in current market interest rates and the remaining time to maturity/redemption
- in the case of convertibles and participating preferred stock, an equity valuation or common stock valuation, might be regarded as more appropriate.

Highly Leveraged Transactions

In the UK, the British Venture Capital Association recognizes the difficulty of reliable valuations for HLTs, particularly when market interest rates or stock market price/earnings ratios are volatile. The BCVA suggests two possible approaches:

- valuation at cost, unless an exit reasonably can be foreseen by a flotation or trade sale, or unless the company will require a refinancing. In either circumstance, an increase or devaluation of the investment, if material, would be appropriate
- a formula-based valuation.

A formula-based valuation could be appropriate where the financing package was devised by the venture capitalist or banking advisers. The formula is to

- assess a notional figure for profit. The profit figure should be calculated by estimating profits before interest and tax, minus interest on debt that is not considered excessive. This is the same as the profit before tax, plus interest on debt capital that is considered excessive. An estimated tax charge should then be applied to obtain a notional figure for profits after tax
- value the share capital by applying a price/earnings ratio multiple to the notional profits after tax
- subtract the current value of the excess debt above a normal level
- subtract the current value of preference share capital
- where appropriate, apply a discount to the resulting valuation, to allow for the illiquidity of the shares.

Applying the Valuation Guidelines

These guidelines for investment portfolio valuations are now widely applied. For example, 3i Group in its annual report and accounts includes a profit statement and a balance sheet. The profit statement shows

- income from dividends and interest on investments, less operating costs and administrative expenses, etc.

- the realized profits or losses from the sale of investments
- increases or decreases in the provisions for a rise or fall in value of unrealized investments.

The balance sheet assets consist largely of the current 3i Group investment portfolio, at the company's estimated valuation. 3i Group's policies for investment valuations include the following

- Equity shares and irredeemable preference shares with a stock-market listing, at the mid-market price
- Shares quoted on AIM, at latest trade price less an appropriate discount for illiquidity
- Unquoted equity shares where the company's latest accounts show a profit, at a value estimated by applying to the company's annual earnings a price/earnings ratio multiple appropriate to listed investments of similar companies. For example, if a company's latest after-tax earnings give an earnings per share of £0.20, and a suitable price/earnings ratio for similar listed companies is 12, the basis for the valuation of the investment would be £2.40 per share (£0.20 x 12)
- If the resultant valuation is less than half the book amount of assets, the value is based on half the book assets
- Unquoted equity shares where the company's latest accounts show a loss, at 50% of the net asset value per share, i.e. book value per share, shown in those accounts
- Unquoted equity shares where no accounts have been received in the period following the initial investment, at cost
- Loans and other preference shares, at the lower of cost or recoverable amount.

Where unquoted shares are based on an estimated price/earnings ratio valuation, or on assets, an appropriate discount to reflect unmarketability is then applied.

Valuation policies should be monitored over time, to ensure that they are suitable. 3i Group check the balance sheet value of investments against their sale price when they are eventually realized. So long as the sale value exceeds the balance sheet value, the valuation policy can be judged prudent and therefore either suitable or over-cautious.

Glossary

Bought Deal
Arrangement in which one venture capital organization provides all the required finance for a deal, then sells on or syndicates part of the financing to other organizations after the deal has been completed. Used by large venture capitalists where confidentiality or speed are important.

Bridge Financing
Short-term funding for a buyout or other venture, obtained to complete the deal and subsequently replaced by longer-term funding.

Business Angel
A wealthy individual providing venture capital.

Cap
Clause in a venture capital financing arrangement that sets a maximum limit on the interest rate the borrower will have to pay for (floating rate) funds.

Captive Fund
Venture capital fund owned and funded by a larger group, and that does not raise funds from external sources.

Collar
Clause in a venture capital financing arrangement that sets a maximum and a minimum limit on the interest rate the borrower will pay for (floating rate) funds.

Corporate Venturing
An investment by a large company, either directly or through an investment fund, in a small high-tech company.

Development Capital
Later-stage venture capital finance, provided to a company that is profitable, or

nearly profitable, but that needs funds for further growth and development.

Due Diligence
A detailed investigation by a potential venture capitalist into a company's background, management and business plan.

Earnout
An arrangement in a business purchase deal whereby the seller receives an additional payment at a future date. The size of the payment is based on an agreed formula, typically a multiple of annual earnings of the business in excess of a specified amount.

Equity Kicker
An option to acquire equity in a company at a future date, for example share options and share warrants.

ESOP
Employee share ownership plan. A scheme, usually a trust, established to enable employees to acquire shares in their company at a future date, through the issue of share options.

Exit
The point at which a venture capital organization realizes its investment in a venture by selling its shareholding.

Follow-On Investment
Further investment by the same venture capital organization.

Independent Fund
Venture capital fund that obtains its funds from external investment sources, and is independently managed.

Institutional Buyout (IBO)
A buyout initiated by a venture capital organization rather than by a management team.

Internal Rate of Return (IRR)
The return on an investment, expressed as an average annual yield on the amount invested. Return consists of dividends plus capital gains, e.g. from the eventual sale of the shares.

Junior Debt
Loans that rank after senior debt in entitlement to repayment, in the event of the borrower's business going into liquidation.

Junk Bonds
Unsecured, therefore high-yielding debt securities issued by US companies, perhaps to finance a buyout or buy-in. A secondary market in junk bonds exists in the US. Junk bonds have a non-investment grade credit rating.

Key Man Insurance
Life assurance/accident insurance/serious illness insurance taken out by a venture company on its key personnel.

Lead Investor
Venture capital organization that takes the biggest stake in a venture, and usually arranges the deal, organizes the venture capital syndicate and provides management involvement in the form of board representation on behalf of the syndicate.

Leverage
Ratio of debt capital to equity finance in a company's financial structure.

Leveraged Buyout (LBO)
Buyout financed primarily by debt finance, often with significant involvement by a financial organization and a comparatively small financial stake held by the management team.

Management Buy-In (MBI)
The purchase of a business by an external management team, with the help of financial backers.

Management Buyout (MBO)
The purchase of a business by its existing management, with the help of financial backers.

Mezzanine Finance
Unsecured loans used as part of the financing package for a venture, e.g. a buyout. The loans rank behind senior debt but ahead of equity in the event of the company's failure. The loans often carry an equity kicker as an incentive to the lender.

Newco
Name often given to a new company set up as the vehicle for a buyout. The management team and venture capitalist invest in Newco that buys the target company or business from the seller.

Ratchet
An incentive arrangement for management in a buyout, agreed with their venture capital backers. The management receives a larger share of the equity if the company is successful.

Second-Round Financing
Further financing to a company that has previously obtained venture capital in a first round of financing. Provided to companies that have performed well and need more capital to develop.

Semi-Captive Fund
Venture capital organization that invests funds on behalf of a parent organization but that also raises funds externally that it then manages independently.

Senior Debt
Secured debt.

Slippage
Term referring to the failure of a venture to meet its business plan targets. For example, development costs exceed budget, the development period takes longer than expected, or sales turnover fails to pick up as quickly as originally planned.

Syndicated Investment
Financing arrangement in which several venture capital organizations collaborate to provide the required funds.

Vendor Finance
Financing arrangement for a buyout or buy-in whereby the seller (vendor) provides part of the finance to help with the purchase. Vendor finance could take the form of a loan or a minority stake in the company.

Venture Capital Organization
Organization that provides funds and advice for business ventures.

Index